#FUTUREPROOF:
Edition Six

#PRstack: AI tools for marketing, media and public relations

This #PRstack book describes how AI is being used in marketing, media and public relations and how to incorporate it into your workflow. The book has been crowdsourced from developers and practitioners and includes an overview of more than 20 individual AI tools and platforms.

Edited by Stephen Waddington

Introduction

AN INTRODUCTION TO #FUTUREPROOF AND THE #PRSTACK GUIDE TO AI TOOLS FOR PUBLIC RELATIONS

Sarah Waddington CBE

There has been an explosion of tools based on large language models since the launch of ChatGPT by OpenAI in November last year.

New products are added to databases such as Chiefmartec and Future Tools, and launched daily on ProductHunt, each promising to disrupt workflow and help practitioners work more efficiently.

Developers are driving much of the conversation around AI tools. The energy has yet to be matched by dialogue among the practitioner community about the best way to incorporate tools into the workflow.

This crowdsourced AI #PRstack guide to the public relations market published by #FuturePRoof aims to address this issue. Its goal is to describe the application of various AI tools to help widen understanding and improve ethical adoption.

Each article describes an AI tool. These have all been crowdsourced and written by individual practitioners and developers. Our thanks to everyone who has volunteered their time and got involved.

The book tells how AI is being used across the public relations workflow - from ideation and planning to content creation, media/influencer outreach, reporting and analysis. But human skill is still key for strategy, relationships, and quality control.

Large language models (LLMs) such as ChatGPT and Claude are disrupting public relations by automating and enhancing many public relations tasks and workflows. These AI tools can generate content, analyse data, optimise pitches, track coverage, and more.

Open source LLMs like LLaMA 2 allow organisations to utilise AI while maintaining data security, transparency, and affordability compared to proprietary models. However, technical expertise is needed to implement them.

Tools such as Fireflies and Otter.ai automate administrative tasks such as transcription, media monitoring, and press pitching/tracking to improve efficiency. They streamline content workflows.

Image generation AI like DALL-E, MidJourney and Stable Diffusion are transforming visual content creation for public relations by generating customised images from text prompts. But copyright and bias issues need addressing.

AI writing tools such as Anyword, Copy.ai, Jasper, and OnePitch help draft content at scale for articles, blogs, pitches, press releases and media content. Finally, a new class of tools is aiming to provide end-to-end media relations workflow. This includes Propel, PRophet and Prowly.

I founded #FuturePRoof in 2015 with the aim of promoting the role of public relations as a management discipline. This is our sixth crowdsourced project and seventh book.

#PRstack is a community developed by Frederik Vincx and Stephen Waddington. It has been inactive since 2015 but previously published two guides to tools in public relations.

Sarah Waddington CBE

Sarah Waddington CBE is a director of Wadds Inc. and advises creative agency management teams on company direction to deliver sustainable growth.

A Chartered Director and IoD ambassador, she has over 20 years of experience in helping organisations to articulate their purpose, engage stakeholders, create value and deliver social impact.

Sarah founded the #FuturePRoof community in 2015 in a bid to reassert public relations as a strategic management function. She is also the co-founder of Socially Mobile, a not-for-profit PR training school helping those from lower socio-economic backgrounds and under-represented groups to increase their earning potential.

A pioneer of best practice, her CBE was awarded in June 2021 for services to public relations and voluntary sectors. She was also awarded the CIPR's Sir Stephen Tallents Medal for exceptional achievement in public relations and the PRCA's Outstanding Contribution in Digital Award.

Sarah is a Past President of the CIPR, a PRCA Fellow, a member of the Northern Power Women Power List, features on Provoke Media's Innovator 25 EMEA 2021 list and is a regular speaker at industry events.

If you're interested in exploring issues raised by this latest edition of #FuturePRoof within your organisation through workshops, training or rethinking your workflow, you can contact Sarah at:
Sarah.Waddington@wadds.co.uk.

#FuturePRoof: Edition Six | #PRstack: AI tools for marketing, media and public relations

CONTENTS

An introduction to #FuturePRoof and the #PRstack guide to AI tools for public relations   03
Table of contents   06
Learning objectives   08
Understanding the explosion in AI in public relations tools   09
An overview of the AI tools described in #PRstack   11
Acknowledgements   14
Disclaimer   15

(i) Large language models

CHAPTER 01	Claude *Andrew Bruce Smith*	17
CHAPTER 02	ChatGPT *Ben Lowndes*	22
CHAPTER 03	LLaMA 2 *Laura Richards*	27

(ii) AI productivity tools

CHAPTER 04	Image generative AI *Laura Richards*	33
CHAPTER 05	Bing Image Creator *Claire Simpson*	38
CHAPTER 06	Canva *Lynnea Olivarez*	42
CHAPTER 07	Fireflies *Ann-Marie Blake*	47
CHAPTER 08	Otter.ai *Tom Beswick*	52
CHAPTER 09	Overtone *Christopher Brennan*	57
CHAPTER 10	Jasper *Cherise Glymph*	61
CHAPTER 11	Anyword *Claire Simpson*	65
CHAPTER 12	Copy.ai *Erin Lovett*	70
CHAPTER 13	Wordtune *Ali Yaseen*	74

CHAPTER 14	Taskade *Philippe Borremans*	78
CHAPTER 15	GPT for Sheets *Paul Stollery*	82
CHAPTER 16	Advanced Data Analysis plug-in *James Crawford*	87

(iii) Integrated AI in public relations platforms

CHAPTER 17	BuzzSumo *Louise Linehan*	94
CHAPTER 18	PRophet *Aaron Kwittken*	101
CHAPTER 19	Prowly *Aleksandra Kubicka*	105
CHAPTER 20	OnePitch *Sarah Pekala*	110
CHAPTER 21	Propel *Zach Cutler*	115

Meet the editor — 120

LEARNING OBJECTIVES

Stephen Waddington

This book provides an overview of how different AI tools can be applied across marketing, media and public relations workflow. Its goal is to provide a practitioner-focused overview of AI capabilities for public relations workflow optimisation.

The key learning objectives are set out below:

- Understand how large language models such as Claude and ChatGPT can automate content generation and analysis to boost public relations productivity.

- Learn how open-source models like LLaMA 2 allow customised AI applications with transparency and data security.

- Discover how tools such as Fireflies, Otter.ai, and Overtone automate administrative tasks like transcription, monitoring, and coverage analysis.

- Explore how image generation AI such as DALL-E and Stable Diffusion streamline visual content creation.

- See how writing assistants like Anyword, Copy.ai and Jasper can help draft customised content at scale.

- Recognise how end-to-end public relations tools such as Propel, PRophet and Prowly aim to simplify media pitching, monitoring, and measurement.

- Appreciate the need for human skills in public relations strategy, relationships and quality control when adopting AI tools.

UNDERSTANDING THE EXPLOSION IN AI IN PUBLIC RELATIONS TOOLS

Stephen Waddington

A report published by the CIPR in February 2023 found that the impact of AI on public relations has been limited in the past five years but is set to explode. It identified more than 5,800 tools with applications in public relations workflow but, until very recently, limited application of AI.

The report was researched and written by Andrew Bruce Smith and myself, with support from Professor Emeritus Anne Gregory, Jean Valin, and Scott Brinker.

The CIPR has been at the forefront of exploring the impact of technology on public relations and society over the past 30 years through work on the internet, social media, and most recently AI, data, and machine learning.

Andrew and I originally set out the project's scope in May 2022. The plan was to update a report from five years previous about the tool market for public relations. The report was ready for publication in October. However, the launch of tools based on the GPT-3 dataset led to a complete reappraisal of the project.

The report was a story of two halves. The first half examined the current tool landscape for public relations based on an analysis of the Chiefmartec dataset built by Scott Brinker. The second identified the explosion in communications, public relations, and marketing tools because of the GPT-3 Large Language Model and other related AI-based technologies.

We sought the help of Scott, founder, and editor of the Chiefmartec website, to characterise the tool market for public relations. Scott has built a comprehensive dataset of more than 10,000 tools used in marketing and related fields, including public relations. The Chiefmartec database, published each year since 2011, is an open-source project that invites public submissions.

Our analysis suggested that there are 18 categories, involving around 5,800 tools, that have the potential to be applied to public relations practice ranging from stakeholder management to web analytics, and from content management to project management. We'd encourage you to explore the dataset for yourself.

Up until November 2022, the market for public relations tools has been characterised by point solutions

focused on a specific application. There's limited evidence of integrated solutions. Innovation in tools in public relations, and adoption by practitioners, appeared to have changed little in the past five years.
We can already see that November 2022 was an inflexion point. The rapid arrival and accessibility of a new generation of generative AI and machine learning tools and services, coupled with the relatively easy ability to integrate these technologies, has since created the potential for significant effects on all aspects of public relations practice.

This book was researched and written in September and October 2023. There is an ongoing tension between large language models and third-party developers. Already, we have seen solutions built on top of the AI models such as chatbots, editing, text-generation and summarisation tools, be cannibalised by subsequent generations of AI large language models. The market needs to settle down before serious investments can be made in workflow.

This #PRstack project set out to explore AI tools from both a practitioner and developer perspective. It explores a cross-section of public relations tools and how they are being applied in practice. My thanks to everybody who contributed to the project.

In September of 2023, a CIPR AI in PR panel report authored by Professor Emeritus Anne Gregory, Jean Valin and Dr Swati Virmani titled 'Humans needed more than ever' found that 40% of public relations work is now assisted by AI. No activity has been replaced completely by AI which suggests that, at minimum, oversight is needed for all AI tools.

The report also made the point that public relations is not the sum of all tasks. There is a dimension that is fundamentally human to our work which involves exercising judgement, nuance, an understanding of context, being aware of self and others, all vital to guarding reputation and building relationships. AI tools can't replace humans but it can assist us and save time.

AN OVERVIEW OF THE AI TOOLS DESCRIBED IN #PRSTACK

Large Language Models			
Claude	Large language model-based chatbot developed by Anthropic.		https://claude.ai/chats/
ChatGPT	Large language model-based chatbot developed by OpenAI.		https://openai.com/
LLaMA 2	An open-source large language model developed by Meta.		https://ai.meta.com/llama/
AI productivity tools			
Bing Image Creator	A tool from Microsoft that generates images from text prompts.		https://www.bing.com/create/
DALL-E	Generates images from text descriptions, including original digital art, illustrations and photography.		https://openai.com/dall-e-2/
MidJourney	Generates images, illustrations and animations through text prompts.		https://www.midjourney.com/
Stable Diffusion	Open source tool that produces images and animations from text descriptions.		https://stablediffusionweb.com/

Canva	Graphic design platform for creating professional-level visual content.	https://www.canva.com/
Fireflies	Meeting assistant that generates transcripts, summaries, and action items from audio recordings.	https://fireflies.ai/
Otter.ai	Transcription tool that converts audio from meetings, interviews, and other sources into editable, shareable text.	https://otter.ai/
Overtone	Qualitative analysis of media coverage through automated classification.	https://overtone.ai/
Jasper	A writing tool that helps create content for different channels.	https://www.jasper.ai/
Anyword	A writing tool that generates content for different marketing channels and analyses messaging performance.	https://anyword.com/
Copy.ai	Writing assistant that utilises multiple language models to help generate advertising and marketing content.	https://www.copy.ai/
Wordtune	A writing assistant that helps polish and refine text by suggesting improvements for clarity, conciseness, tone and style.	https://www.wordtune.com/
Taskade	A productivity and collaboration platform that enables teams to manage projects and workflows.	https://www.taskade.com/ai/

GPT for Sheets	A plugin that brings the power of ChatGPT to Google Sheets that uses AI to analyse data, reformat content, and automate repetitive tasks.	https://workspace.google.com/marketplace/app/gpt_for_sheets_and_docs/677318054654
OpenAI Advanced Data Analysis plug-in	A data analysis tool that enables non-coders to analyse data and gain insights.	https://openai.com/

Integrated AI in public relations platforms

BuzzSumo	A platform that helps find journalists, analyse content engagement, build media lists, draft personalised pitches, and monitor the impact of coverage.	https://buzzsumo.com/
PRophet	A generative and predictive AI SaaS platform that creates, analyses and tests content that predicts earned media interest and sentiment.	https://www.prprophet.ai/
Prowly	A platform that assists with drafting releases, discovering media contacts, email pitching, media monitoring and coverage reporting.	https://prowly.com/
OnePitch	A pitching platform that helps create targeted media lists, improve pitch quality with feedback, and track interactions with journalists.	https://onepitch.co/
Propel	A platform that helps generate content, identify media targets, personalise pitches, monitor coverage, and analyse ROI to streamline earned media activities.	https://www.propelmypr.com/

ACKNOWLEDGEMENTS

Our thanks to the following people for their help and support with this project:

Tom Bestwick, Ann-Marie Blake, Philippe Borremans, Christopher Brennan, Scott Brinker, James Crawford, Eitan Goldstein, Professor Emeritus Anne Gregory, Aleksandra Kubicka, Ben Lowndes, Louise Linehan, Erin Lovett, Tara Maupai, Lynnea Olivarez, Sarah Pekala, Laura Richards, Claire Simpson, Andrew Bruce Smith, Paul Stollery, Ali Yaseen, Dr Swati Virman and Jean Valin.

DISCLAIMER

This book was created through crowdsourcing, where numerous individuals contributed content via the internet. The editor and publisher have made efforts to ensure the accuracy of the information presented, but cannot guarantee that the content is free from errors or omissions.

The information provided should not be understood as professional advice. The contributors, editors, and publisher disclaim all warranties with regard to the information provided, including implied warranties of merchantability and fitness for a particular purpose. The use of this book and the content provided is at the reader's sole risk. The contributors, editors, and publisher shall not be liable for any damages arising from the use of this book, whether direct, indirect, special, incidental or consequential.

The views expressed in this book are those of the contributors and editors and do not necessarily represent the views of the publisher. The inclusion of links, accounts, opinions or advice of contributors does not imply endorsement by the editors or publisher.

This book is provided for informational purposes only. The editor and publisher do not warrant or make any representations regarding the use, interpretation, or application of information contained in the book.

In no event shall the editor or publisher be liable for any direct, indirect, consequential, special, exemplary or other damages arising from the use of this book.

(i)

LARGE LANGUAGE MODELS

#FuturePRoof: Edition Six

CHAPTER
01

CHAPTER **01**

CLAUDE

Andrew Bruce Smith | Practitioner

Claude AI is a conversational AI assistant from Anthropic that leverages a large context window, enabling it to excel at processing, summarising, and integrating large volumes of information to bring new capabilities to public relations workflow.

Claude AI is a next-generation conversational AI assistant developed by Anthropic, an artificial intelligence company focused on building helpful, honest, and harm-free AI systems. First released in April 2022, Claude represents a major advance in natural language processing capabilities while prioritising safety, accuracy, and transparency.

At its core, Claude leverages Anthropic's own large language model called Claude 2, allowing it to understand and generate nuanced, high-quality text. Claude 2 was trained on a diverse dataset of internet text and books using Constitutional AI to minimise harmful responses. As a result, Claude claims to provide significantly more accurate, on-topic, and harmless answers than other AI assistants.

Public relations workflow integration

Claude AI can be a very useful tool for public relations practitioners. Like ChatGPT, Claude can generate content like press releases, website copy, or social media posts tailored to specific audiences. However, its key strength lies in its large (75,000 word) context window. In other words, Claude can receive, analyse and return very large amounts of information. Claude is also capable of ingesting information in a wide variety of file formats, such as PDFs, spreadsheets, and presentations.

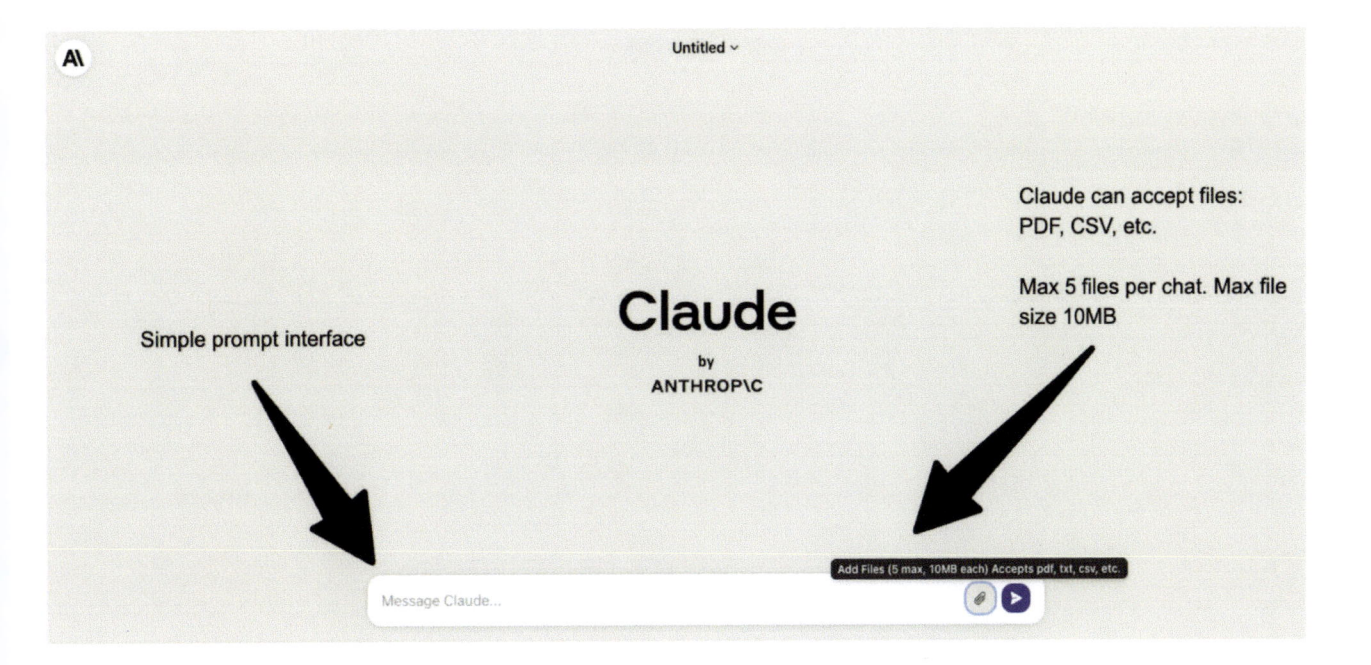

Key benefits of Claude's large context window for public relations practitioners include:

- **Comprehensive analysis**
The large context window allows Claude to process extensive documents like research papers, legal briefs, and annual reports. This provides a more complete understanding of complex materials compared to only analysing text snippets. Example use cases include generating first-draft communication plans and pitch responses based on providing all necessary background information and objectives to the AI to allow it to assimilate, analyse and generate an initial recommendation.

- **Text summarisation**
Claude can digest and summarise large volumes of text, condensing books, articles, or documents into concise overviews. This makes it easy to grasp key information quickly.

- **Knowledge integration**
Claude excels at combining information from different sources into a synthesised answer, showcasing strong reading comprehension.

- **Improved reasoning**
With more context available, Claude can better reason about concepts and connections within large bodies of information. This leads to more accurate and nuanced responses.

- **Natural conversations**

The large context window enables Claude to maintain context across long dialogues without "forgetting" earlier parts of the discussion. This facilitates more natural back-and-forth conversations.

- **Creative writing**

Claude can generate longer and more coherent content thanks to the expanded context. This makes Claude better suited for creative writing applications.

- **Multitasking**

The increased context size allows Claude to effectively switch between various tasks and topics during a conversation while retaining relevant information.

The significantly expanded 75,000-word context window empowers Claude to fully utilise its advanced natural language capabilities when processing large volumes of information. This enables a wide range of beneficial applications for public relations tasks that are not easily achievable with more limited context sizes.

Claude is currently available through a free web-based chat interface that allows open-ended conversations. Users can also access Claude through a developer API to integrate its capabilities into other applications.

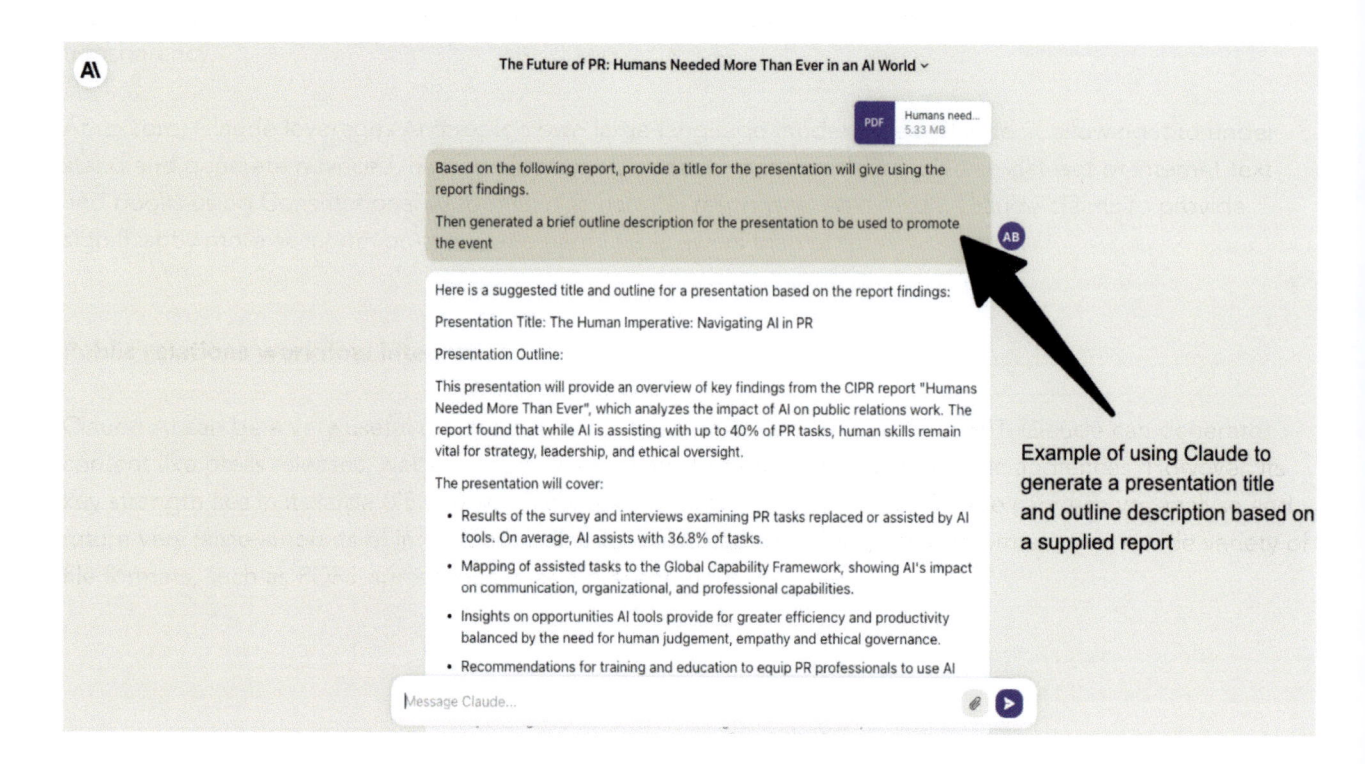

Example of using Claude to generate a presentation title and outline description based on a supplied report

In September 2023, Anthropic launched Claude Pro, a paid subscription tier offering priority access even during high-demand periods. Claude Pro also unlocks additional features as they are released.

Looking ahead, Anthropic plans to continue expanding Claude's knowledge and skills to handle more advanced tasks. With its constitutional AI approach as a guiding framework, the company aims to usher in a new generation of AI that balances wide-ranging intelligence with robust safety.

Its conversational ability, knowledge integration, harm avoidance, and speed set it apart as one of the most capable and trustworthy AI agents available today. As Claude continues its rapid development, it may well become an integral part of how public relations practitioners leverage and apply AI to their day-to-day workflows.

Andrew Bruce Smith, founder, Escherman
https://www.linkedin.com/in/andrewbrucesmith/

Andrew Bruce Smith is a renowned expert in artificial intelligence and its applications in digital comms, social media, SEO, and analytics. He is Chair of the CIPR's AI in PR panel, and a sought-after consultant, trainer, conference speaker and commentator on the impact of AI on the public relations industry.

#FuturePRoof: Edition Six

CHAPTER
02

CHAPTER **02**

CHATGPT

Ben Lowndes | Practitioner

ChatGPT is an AI tool that offers transformative potential for public relations activities like ideation, content creation, analysis and reporting, but users must invest time to understand its capabilities, refine prompts carefully, and apply quality controls.

When considering AI's impact on working life, it's easy to overlook that ChatGPT hasn't had its first birthday at the time of writing.

User numbers shot past 100m in less than three months at the start of 2023. This set the foundations for the biggest disruption to public relations practice since social media's arrival a generation ago.

Whatever area of public relations you work in, ChatGPT can support stages of activity ranging from ideation to content creation, delivery, reporting and analysis.

Nuts and bolts of ChatGPT

Part of OpenAI's suite of tools, ChatGPT uses machine learning to analyse and generate text responses to users' input (or 'prompts').

The application can answer questions, write in the style of a professional or well-known individual and engage in conversation about a topic.

While its content generation capability attracts wide interest, its ability to condense detail into summary form is arguably more useful for time-pressed comms people striving to simplify complex information and provide content for different channels.

That said, practitioners won't get decent outputs without the right input and refinements based on their professional judgement.

How to use it

Users can access various versions on chat.openai.com. A free version, ChatGPT-3, has basic features. A monthly subscription to ChatGPT-4 (currently $20 per user) offers priority access and faster response times. Businesses can also use API (Application Programming Interface) access, enabling ChatGPT's integration with other software and services.

When setting up, there are 'custom instructions' to tailor ChatGPT's responses to your needs. If, for example, you wish to avoid Americanisms, and focus on a particular industry, you can use these instructions to set such expectations.

To use ChatGPT:

- Type your 'prompt' or question into the box at the bottom of this image. Be clear about what you're asking, and what you don't want. Provide detail – about audiences, industries and markets – to focus the response.
- Click 'generate'.
- Check that the output is accurate and refine it accordingly.

Using ChatGPT-4, you can also upload documents and data to shape your responses at this stage.

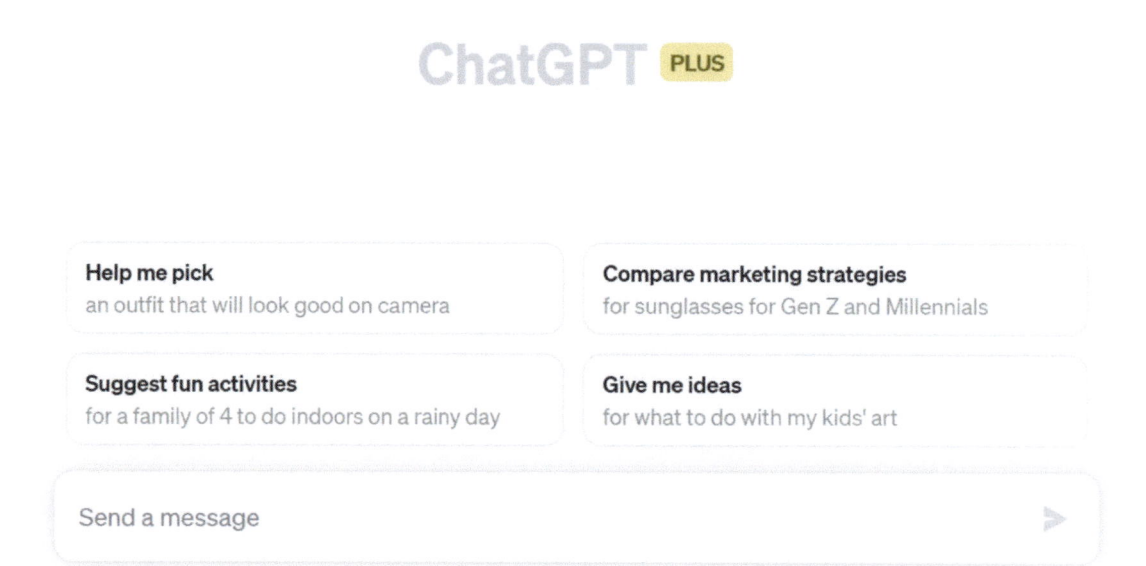

Example use cases

ChatGPT can potentially support a huge range of tasks. Here are some options to illustrate how it could support public relations work.

For planning, ask for:

- Campaign ideas to help a [business/product/brand] promote its [offer / USP] in [market]. Say you want themes, not tactics or an explanation of what's needed.
- PESTLE and SWOT analysis for a scenario to support research.

For delivery, ask for:

- Repurposed content: produce a statement, press release or series of social media posts from the information provided. Set the audience, channels, length and format.
- Analyse [information/data]. Summarise [xxx] words for [newsletter/website].
- Threaded social media posts from content provided.

For reporting and evaluation, ask for:

- Analyse [comments or feedback] and break down positive, negative and neutral comments.
- Themes and issues relating to [data/info]. This image represents how this could work in response to a prompt asking for themes and issues on a (totally fictitious!) social listening exercise.

Trends and Patterns

1. **General Topics**: The dataset reveals that the most frequent words in the content are often general terms like "RT" (retweet). This indicates high engagement but lacks focus on specific topics or themes.
2. **Primary Source of Discussion**: A large portion of mentions come from one particular social media platform, indicating its importance as a primary channel for discussions.
3. **Type of Engagement**: Most posts are categorised as "engagements," which include actions like retweets and replies. This suggests that there is more interaction with existing content rather than the creation of new, original posts.

Final considerations

While offering introductory thoughts on how ChatGPT can support public relations activity, this post doesn't even start to scratch the surface.

As with any tool, it's key to invest time in understanding what it can and can't do, and discuss with colleagues how to implement it best.

Having quality control measures in place is also vital. ChatGPT can go wild and produce false information. Your judgement and adherence to accuracy is a counterweight to this. If using it to analyse data, ensure you comply with GDPR and respect confidentiality.

And finally, and perhaps most importantly, there's no substitute for testing and tweaking your approach to find ways that work for you.

Ben Lowndes, founder, Distinctive Communications
https://www.linkedin.com/in/blowndes

Ben founded Distinctive Communications in 2022 after working in journalism and public relations for more than 20 years. A dad to two teenagers, he's created and delivered communication strategies for local and national governments, charities, universities, and businesses.

#FuturePRoof: Edition Six

CHAPTER 03

CHAPTER **03**

LLAMA 2

Laura Richards | Practitioner

Open-source large language models such as Meta's LLaMA 2 enable organisations to run AI on their own infrastructure for customised applications in public relations, providing transparency, affordability, data security, and tailoring while requiring technical expertise for implementation.

Alongside well-known Large Language Models (LLMs), such as OpenAI's GPT and Google's Bard, sits an alternative for organisations looking to utilise deep learning models. Open-source LLMs use the same type of neural networks and large data sets to train AI models to understand and generate different types of content, but they make their source code and training models available publicly. The most well-publicised open-source LLM is Meta's LLaMA 2 (released July '23).

LLaMA 2 has three core options (models) to generate human-like text: its main pre-trained model, plus two fine-tuned models focusing on 'chat' and 'coding'. The LLM's performance is on a par with comparable proprietary models, having been trained on a colossal amount of text sourced from the web, including platforms like Wikipedia and Project Gutenberg. For the release of Llama 2, the training data was curated to remove websites that often disclose users' personal data, and weighted its sampling towards trustworthy sources.

Where it fits within public relations workflow

Unlike proprietary LLMs, open-source models don't require a licence and can be used, modified and distributed by anyone. They are also free to use (although infrastructure costs are associated with running them). The downside is that they do not have a user-friendly interface available off-the-shelf, so we are unlikely to see individuals starting to use LLaMA 2 in their everyday workflows in the way that large models such as ChatGPT have been adopted.

The opportunity for agencies and in-house teams is that open-source LLMs can be used within a company's own digital infrastructure, providing complete control over company data and reducing the risk of data leaks and unauthorised access. Once set up, open-source LLMs can also be trained on company data, or trained to carry out specific tasks. This means that public relations agencies and teams can benefit from:

- Transparent AI models.
- That are affordable.
- That offer data security and confidentiality.
- That can be tailored to the company's needs.

As of the time of writing, large enterprises are more likely than smaller agencies to start embedding LLaMA 2/ open source LLMs into their workflow, due to the technical know-how required to train and maintain a bespoke AI. However, this might change as new tools and software services are built on top of LLaMA 2, making its capabilities more accessible to public relations practitioners.

How to use LLaMA 2

Anyone who wants to try LLaMA 2 can do so at llama2.ai, a chatbot demo that is available publicly.

For organisations or individuals that want to run LLaMA 2 on their own machines or within their own cloud infrastructure, they will need to download the code from Hugging Face (the leading platform for open-source AI models). This requires a Hugging Face account (free) and the necessary libraries and dependencies to run the code. For organisations that do not have an in-house technical team, hiring a developer that understands AI is the easiest way to get started.

meta-llama/Llama-2-7b-chat-hf

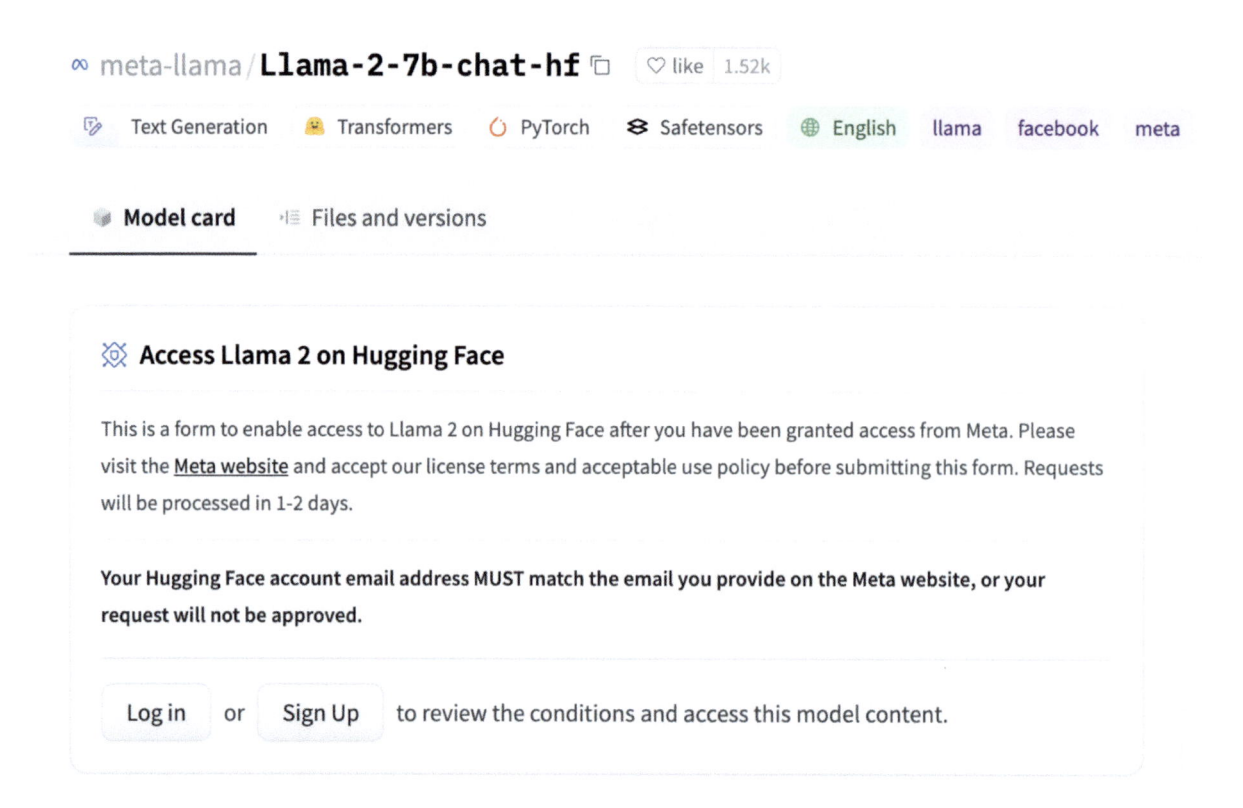

Text Generation · Transformers · PyTorch · Safetensors · English · llama · facebook · meta

Model card · Files and versions

⚛ Access Llama 2 on Hugging Face

This is a form to enable access to Llama 2 on Hugging Face after you have been granted access from Meta. Please visit the Meta website and accept our license terms and acceptable use policy before submitting this form. Requests will be processed in 1-2 days.

Your Hugging Face account email address MUST match the email you provide on the Meta website, or your request will not be approved.

[Log in] or [Sign Up] to review the conditions and access this model content.

LLaMA 2 can also be accessed directly through Microsoft Azure and Amazon Web Services.

Example use cases

- **Tailored customer service**

Imagine having a virtual assistant who can answer customer inquiries around the clock, trained on the content of a company website or other proprietary materials. This way, when customers or potential clients ask questions, they would interact with a chatbot that understands the company's offerings and responds in a natural, engaging manner. It makes personalised customer service available 24/7.

- **Knowledge repositories**

Onboarding new staff can be time-consuming, especially when familiarising them with company-specific information. LLaMA 2 can be used to create internal chatbots or knowledge bases that hold answers to common company-related questions. New team members can ask the chatbot about company policies, project procedures, or any other relevant information, and get instant, accurate answers.

- **Advanced data analytics**

Evaluating the success of campaigns often involves sifting through loads of data, which can be daunting - especially for those not well-versed with data analysis. LLaMA 2 can simplify this process by allowing public relations practitioners to interact with data in a conversational manner. For instance, instead of wrestling with complex analytics tools, you could simply ask the system to summarise the key takeaways from a recent campaign, analyse web traffic data, or gauge the sentiment of press coverage.

Laura Richards, founder, Idea Junkies
https://www.linkedin.com/in/laurarichardsfcipr/

Laura Richards is a public relations practitioner and founder of Idea Junkies, an agency championing ideas that change the world. She is a technology enthusiast who spends her spare time building AI tools with NoCode.

(ii)

AI PRODUCTIVITY TOOLS

#FuturePRoof: Edition Six

CHAPTER 04

CHAPTER **04**

IMAGE GENERATIVE AI

Laura Richards | Practitioner

Image-generating AI tools such as DALL-E, MidJourney, and Stable Diffusion enable public relations practitioners to create visual assets from text prompts, but raise concerns about copyright, bias, and ethical use.

Image-generating Generative AI applies the same foundation models as other types of LLMs, but instead of producing written content, it produces visual content. Popular platforms include Stable Diffusion, MidJourney and OpenAI's DALL-E, although new tools are being released all the time.

Image generative AI allows users to create and manipulate visual content based on text descriptions. The latest versions can create original, realistic illustrations, photography, and digital art from a written prompt, combining concepts, attributes, and styles. They can also make realistic edits to existing images and create variations - for example, blending two images together or turning a photograph into an illustration.

While the technology can create original digital imagery, some artists have accused the companies behind the most popular platforms of using their works to train AI models, without permission. At the time of writing, the legal cases are still being decided, but this raises questions about the derivative nature of AI-generated imagery and the protection of artists' original works.

There are other challenges and ethical considerations that practitioners should be aware of. The technology has been criticised for having a built-in bias, with images often drawing on or perpetuating racist tropes. There have also been instances of these tools being used to create deep fake non-consensual pornography. The main platforms are trying to mitigate these risks by introducing safety measures and off-setting biased datasets.

Where it fits within the public relations workflow

The potential applications of image generating Generative AI in the public relations industry sit firmly in the design and content creation space. These tools can help public relations practitioners create engaging visual content for campaigns, social media, and presentations, all based on simple text descriptions. AI can aid in all three stages of visual content creation - brainstorming, creation, and editing.

How to use image generation AI

DALL-E

The latest version of OpenAI's DALL-E can be accessed for free via Microsoft Bing Image Creator (Microsoft account needed) and through ChatGPT for users with a Plus account. Users simply type out the image they want to see, including any style references (e.g. illustration, watercolour, vector, HD photo, etc) and DALL-E will return a selection of images.

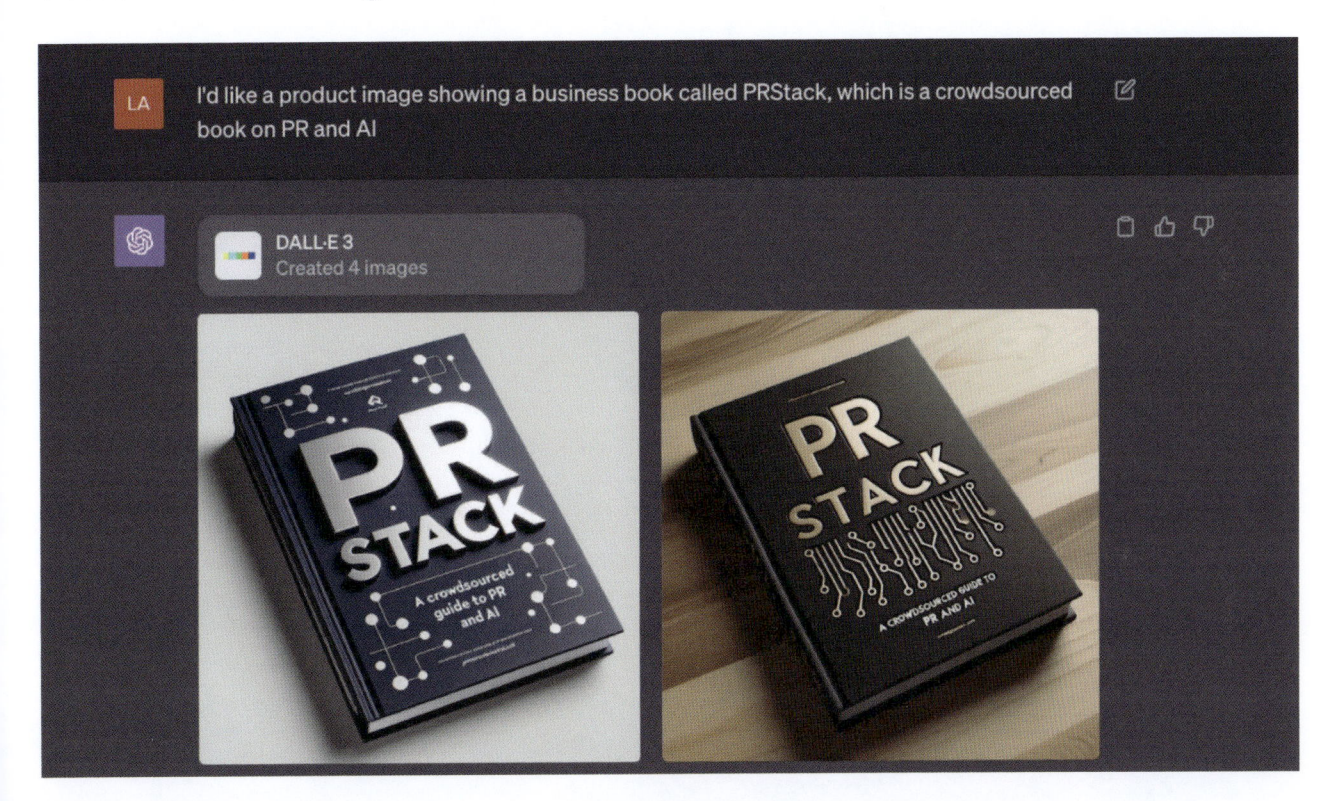

MidJourney

MidJourney runs on the decentralised chat service Discord. The free and premium versions can be accessed by joining the MidJourney Server. Commands are given in community rooms or through direct messages with the MidJourney bot. Core commands include:

/imagine - tells MidJourney to create an image based on the provided prompt.
/blend - tells MidJourney to mix two images together.
/describe - creates a prompt for an image the user uploads.

Users are also able to add the MidJourney bot to their own servers through the Discord App Directory.

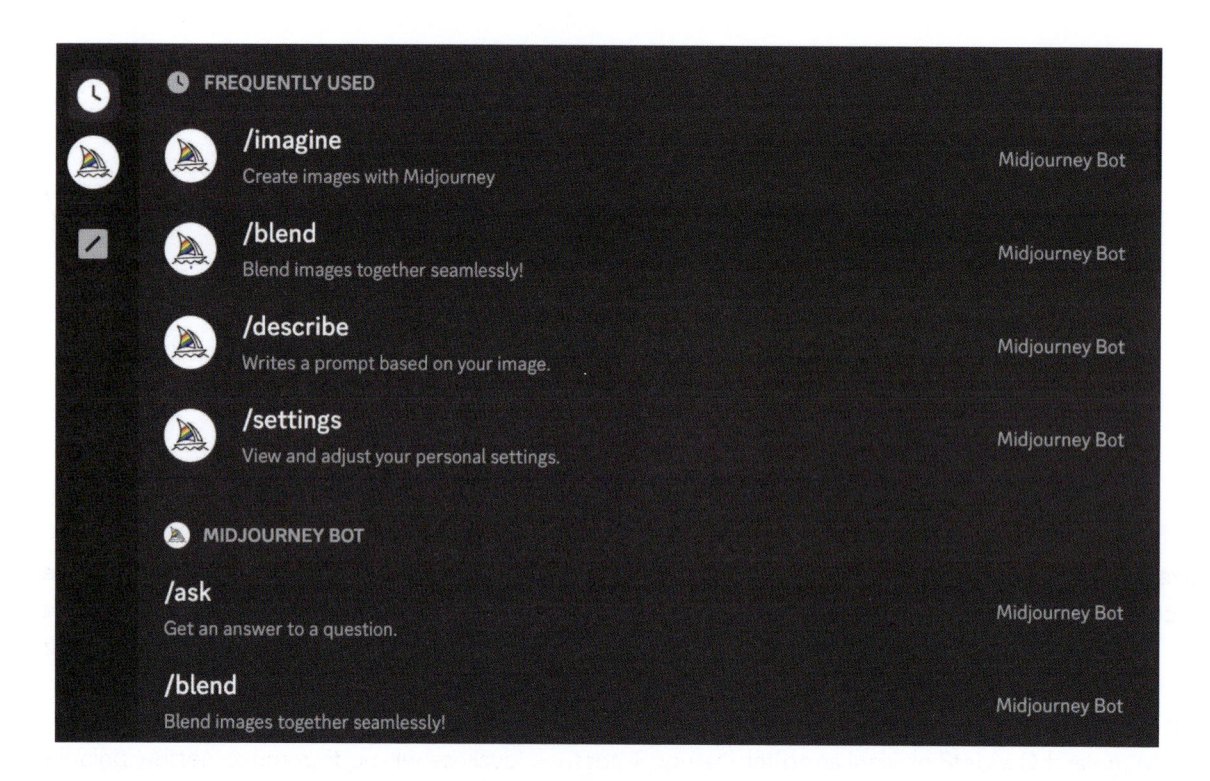

Stable Diffusion

Stable Diffusion is the most flexible AI image generator, allowing users more control over the style of images it generates. It's also open source, meaning it's possible to train it using proprietary datasets. There are two main ways to access Stable Diffusion: the first is by downloading Stable Diffusion and running it on a local device. The second (and simpler option) is to use Clipdrop, the official demo from makers Stability AI.

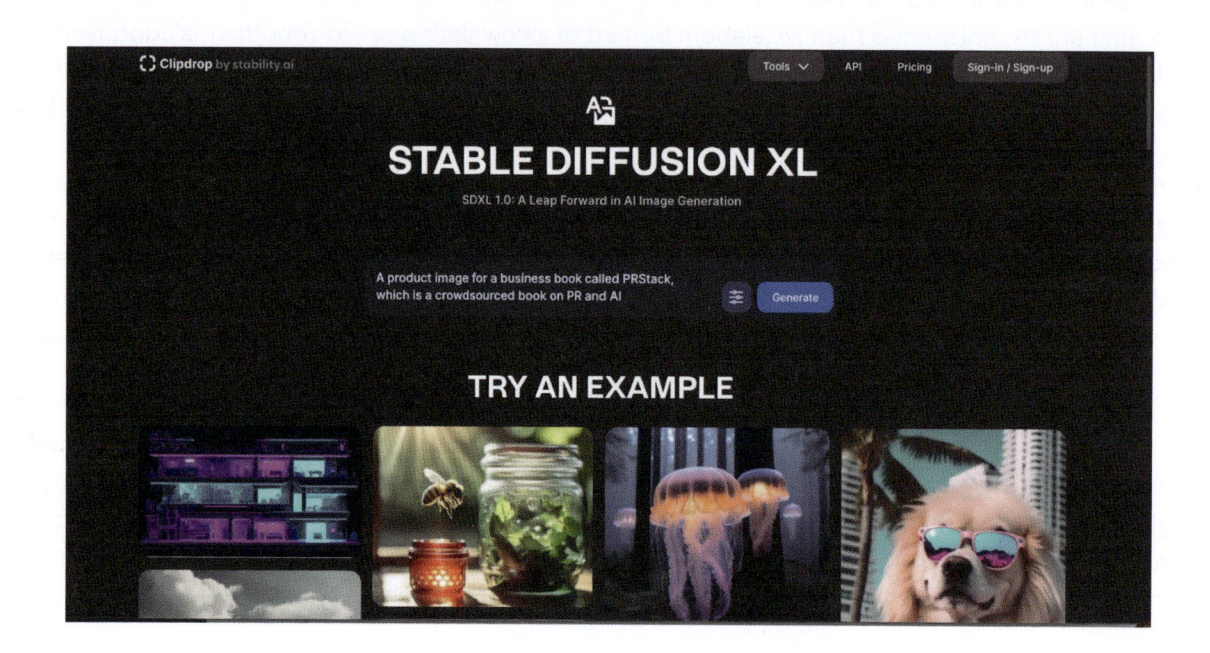

Image-generating generative AI is rapidly being rolled out and embedded in third-party software and websites. For example, Adobe has added a Gen Fill function to Photoshop, while stock image site Getty Images has launched its own version, trained on its own images. Expect to see more companies start to offer image-generation AI, either by embedding tools like Stable Diffusion and DALL-E into their products or by launching their own generative AI models.

Example use cases

- **Visual content creation**

The most obvious use case for image generative AI is to create engaging images for campaigns and content marketing. Generative AII can be used to produce memes, stock imagery, product mock-ups and more.

- **Branded imagery**

Generative AI can be used to create brand-specific content, drawing on specific colour palettes or visual styles. Companies that are willing to spend time training an AI model on their own branded content will see the best results, but practitioners can achieve good results by developing a set of 'brand prompts' to ensure a consistent output.

- **Touch-ups and revisions**

Both standalone Generative AI such as DALL-E and embedded tools such as Photoshop's Gen Fill function, allow users to touch up or change existing imagery. From changing the colour of someone's jacket to filling in an empty space with a specific object, image editing can now be done with a text prompt.

- **Brainstorming (brand identities, concept art, logos)**

Generative AI can help people without a design background come up with ideas for brand identities and logos, or concept art for campaigns. While earlier models of image-generating GenAI struggled if text was needed on an image, the release of OpenAI's DALL-E3 saw significant improvements in this area.

Laura Richards, founder, Idea Junkies
https://www.linkedin.com/in/laurarichardsfcipr/

Laura Richards is a public relations practitioner and founder of Idea Junkies, an agency championing ideas that change the world. She is a technology enthusiast who spends her spare time building AI tools with NoCode.

#FuturePRoof: Edition Six

CHAPTER
05

CHAPTER **05**

BING IMAGE CREATOR

Claire Simpson | Practitioner

Bing Image Creator uses AI to generate visuals from text prompts, offering new creative capabilities for public relations practitioners but raising copyright considerations around AI-produced content.

Bing Image Creator is a text-to-image AI tool, which runs on Open AI's DALL-E model. Using a text prompt, it generates a visual representation of a given description.

The tool is free, though you must sign in with or create a Microsoft account. Like many generative AI tools, credit limits apply. However, these are generous when compared with similar tools in the text-to-image category.

Users receive 25 credits - known as boosts - when they use the tool. These get replenished weekly. Every prompt that a user gives the tool costs one boost. When you run out of boosts, you can still use Image Creator but it will take longer to generate images after you've given it a prompt - usually several minutes. Users also have the option to redeem Microsoft Rewards for extra boosts.

Microsoft has recently integrated Open AI's DALL-E 3 model into Image Creator.

Where it fits within public relations workflow

As a text-to-image tool, Image Creator can support design and creative workstreams. Typically, these tools fit into public relations practice similarly to how stock image libraries are currently used. But as these tools grow more sophisticated, and take on extra functions, so will their use cases in public relations.

How to use it

1. To access Bing Image Creator, head to bing.com/create
2. Click 'Join and Create' to sign in or register with a Microsoft account.
3. Once logged in, simply input a description of an image you want to create in the prompt bar. Then click 'Create'. Image Creator will generate a set of four images that match your given prompt.
4. Click on an image to share, save, or download it. If the results aren't what you were looking for, you can re-enter a refined prompt or input a new one.
5. You can also click the 'Surprise Me' button to generate an example prompt. This can be useful when first experimenting with the tool or learning how to tailor your prompts.
6. The tool currently supports English-language prompts only. Bing has said it is working to support additional languages in future.
7. For optimal results, Bing advises users to be 'highly descriptive' with their prompts. This includes using adjectives describing desired colours, locations, and artistic style. For example, 'digital art', 'illustration', 'photorealistic' etc.

Example use cases of Image Creator include

- **Stock image generation**
Creating highly customisable images for use in pitch decks, blogs or social media assets.

- **Visual explainers**

Turning product descriptions or campaign ideas into illustrations. This can aid public relations practitioners in visual storytelling.

- **Ad renders**

Creating ad renders and concepts for pitching. Ad and creative agencies have already begun using text-to-image tools for mock-ups. This process could take a creative designer a few hours to stitch together from stock images in the past. With tools like Image Creator, it now only takes a few minutes.

While the use cases for text-to-image tools are undeniable, copyright considerations apply. AI-generated image copyright varies across different geographies and jurisdictions and is fast evolving. Potential infringements arise from the use of images that resemble existing copyrighted work. This can result from AI producing similar outputs to the images accessed in its training data.

Claire Simpson, associate director, Hard Numbers
https://www.linkedin.com/in/claire-simpson/

Claire is associate director at performance-driven marketing and public relations consultancy, Hard Numbers. A member of the CIPR's AI in PR Panel, she is keen to educate public relations practitioners on the challenges and opportunities AI technology presents.

CHAPTER 06

CHAPTER **06**

CANVA

Lynnea Olivarez | Practitioner

Canva is an accessible graphic design platform with AI features that enable anyone to easily create professional visuals, making it a versatile tool for handling diverse design needs in public relations workflows.

Canva, launched in 2012, is a graphic design platform enabling users to craft professional designs with no prior experience, thanks to its assortment of customisable templates, fonts, images, and now, AI features. It has democratised design by being accessible and affordable, making it a staple in communications and public relations toolkits. It's widely used, with proficiency in Canva becoming a sought-after skill in contemporary roles.

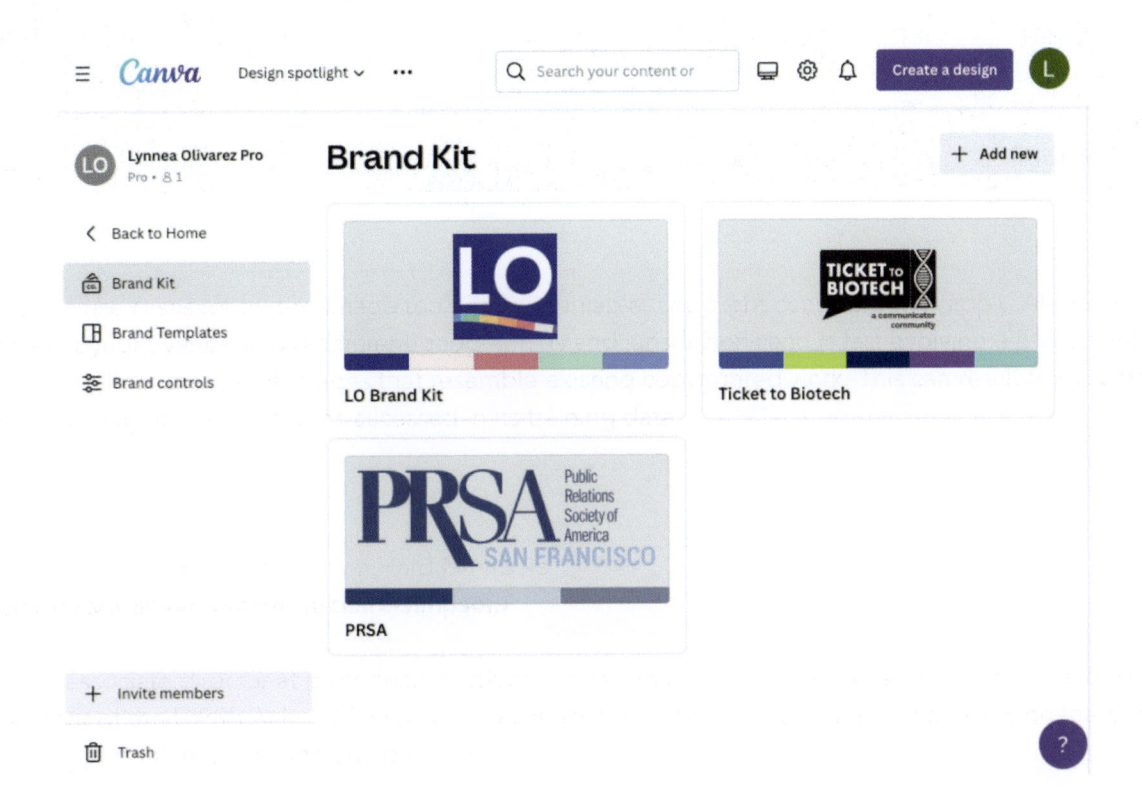

Everyday uses

Canva is constantly changing – and improving. Developers regularly unveil new "magical" features influenced by feedback from its substantial user base of 135 million people across 190 countries. In March 2023, Canva introduced its initial suite of AI-based features, and as of October 2023, Canva launched new tools as part of its one-stop-shop Magic Studio:

- Magic Write: AI-powered writing assistant for content creation, such as for blogs, emails, and YouTube videos.
- Magic Edit: Simplifies the addition or modification of design elements.
- Magic Eraser: Removes objects from photos with a click.
- Magic Design: Provides custom designs and a range of style selections from uploaded images.
- Text-to-Image: Converts word prompts to images with enhanced resolution and styles (upgraded 2022 tool).
- Magic Presentation: Produces initial drafts of presentations, including outlines and content.
- Beat Sync: Helps you create visuals that match the beat of audio in videos.
- Animate: Lets you custom-animate your elements to tell a story.
- Magic Switch: Convert designs into other formats effortlessly, and auto-translate them into over 100 languages for global campaigns.
- Magic Media: Utilise AI to turn text or images into short videos.
- Magic Grab and Magic Expand: Select, edit, and enlarge an image part beyond its frame, akin to a tool Adobe offers.

(Sources: Bootcamp.com, Zapier, Medium, EducatorsTechnology.com, Makeuseof.com, GrowingYourCraft.com, PromptEngineering.org, Great Ai Prompts, Canva)

How Canva works

Canva's web-based tool and mobile app come with a freemium model, offering both free and paid versions, which easily can scale for team design creation and sharing. The platform's extensive reach is also due to its integration with over 150 apps in the Canva App Marketplace, empowering public relations practitioners to publish designs directly to social media or save them to an external file-sharing site, for example. Canva also has recently partnered with DALL·E by OpenAI and Imagen by Google Cloud to enhance its Text-to-Image AI generation features.

Example use cases

Canva's practical applications are expansive, covering various domains in communication workflows. Here are a few use cases:

- Generate a variety of brand kits and templates for corporate, personal, and product brands.
- Optimise social media branding, campaigns, graphics, GIFs, and video files to meet varying channel

parameters.
- Develop professional PowerPoint decks, such as for presenting communication strategies or new business pitch decks.
- Craft promotional materials, invites, or signage for events like webinars or client grand openings.
- Design internal digital signage or intranet graphics.
- Assemble comprehensive media kits for pitch letters or to accompany press release wire distributions.
- Produce website imagery, icons, and page banners.
- Compile stylised media clip books, complete with executive summaries and key takeaways.

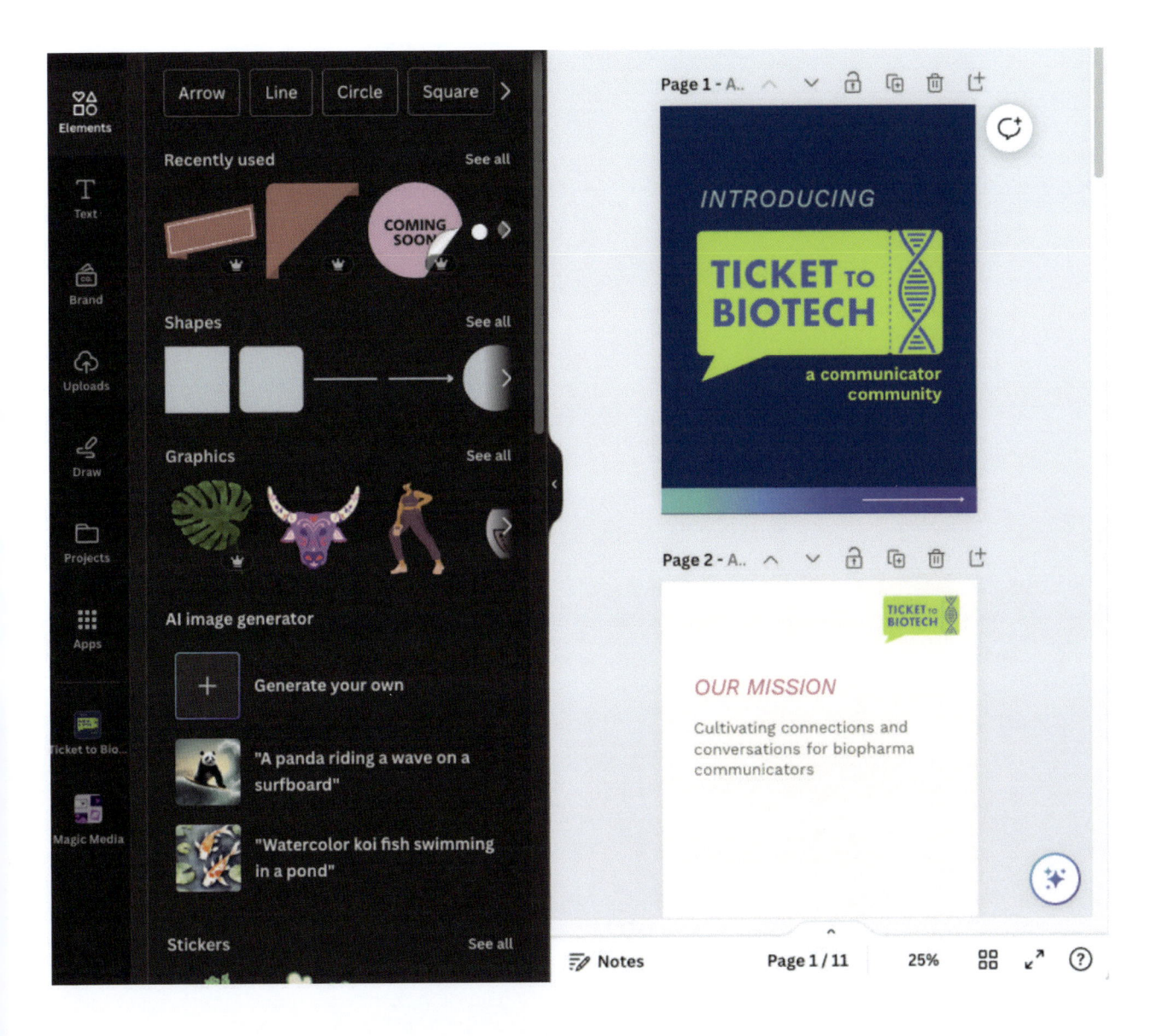

Canva's constant innovations and user-friendly interface make it a versatile tool, aiding in diverse design needs across different communication disciplines. Its ongoing enhancements and collaborations ensure its continued relevance and utility in the public relations tool stack.

Lynnea Olivarez, founder and community manager, Ticket to Biotech
https://www.linkedin.com/in/lynneaolivarez/

A versatile life science communicator with a rich background in leading communications for emerging biotech therapeutics companies, Lynnea specialises in integrated public relations, digital and social media, and employee engagement initiatives. She is currently focused on fostering the new global biopharma communicator community, Ticket to Biotech (T2B), while contributing actively to professional societies, speaking at industry conferences, and mentoring aspiring public relations practitioners.

CHAPTER 07

CHAPTER **07**

FIREFLIES

Ann-Marie Blake | Practitioner

Fireflies uses artificial intelligence technology to transcribe and summarise online meetings and audio recordings. Its capabilities go beyond automated note taking to provide detailed analytics and sentiment analysis.

I've been using Fireflies for two months and already love it. It's easy to get started - just go to the Fireflies ai website, answer a couple of basic questions, and choose a plan to suit your needs. I started with the 'free forever' plan which gave me 800 minutes per month, but soon upgraded to Pro for more minutes and features.

How it works

Fred, the Fireflies Bot, joins your online meeting as a guest and silently sits in the background recording the meeting and taking notes. It's compatible with the popular meeting platforms. I've used it with Microsoft Teams, Zoom and Google Meet with no issues. Meetings must last between 3 -120 minutes for the ai transcription to work.

As part of the terms of service users must let participants know that the call is being recorded. You can either do this verbally at the start of the meeting or configure your settings so that Fireflies does this automatically.

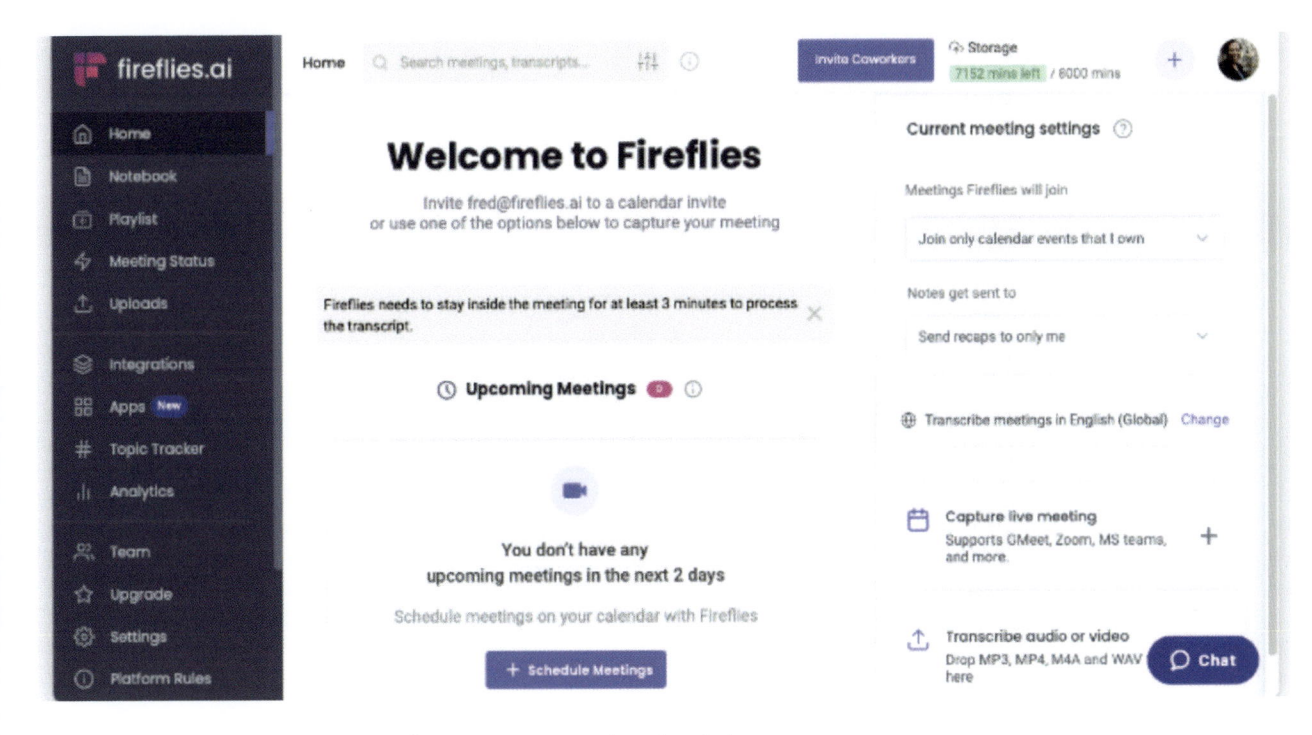

Shortly after the meeting you will receive an email with a link to:

- A summary of the meeting.
- A timeline with timestamps for easy reference.
- A list of suggested action items for follow up.

Even in meetings where English is not the first language for all participants, I've been impressed with the accuracy of the transcript and summaries generated.

Fireflies can be used for in-person meetings but you'll need to record separately and upload a recording to Fireflies so that it can be transcribed using the Fireflies transcription tool.

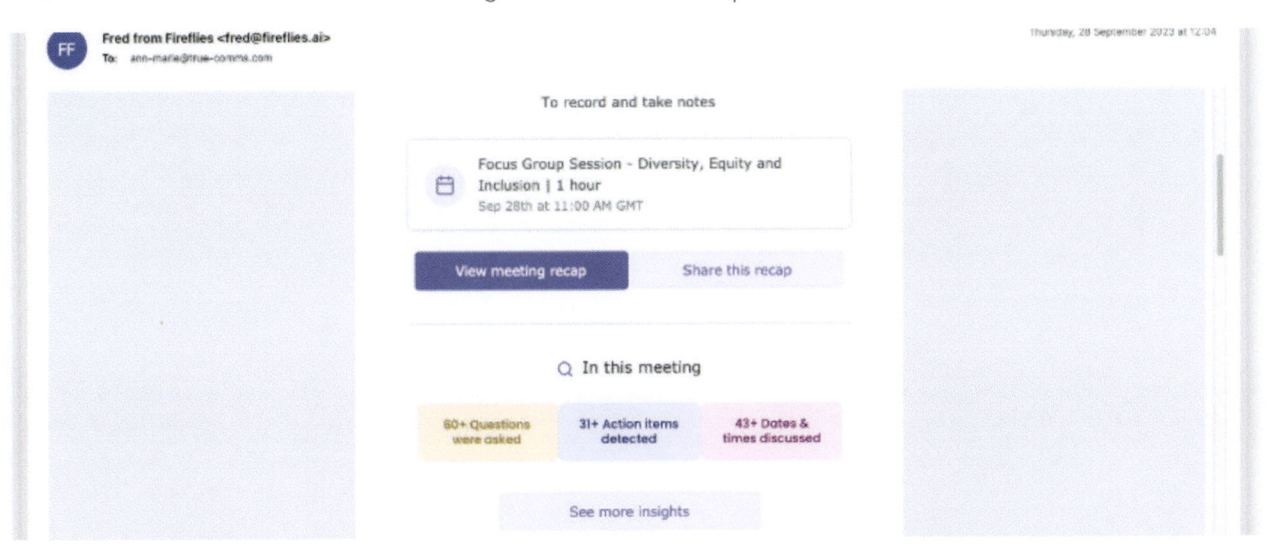

Where it fits within the public relations workflow

Capturing meeting minutes and actions.

Meetings are an essential part of our work in Public Relations but they can often be a source of inefficiency. Whether it's the time taken to manually type up written notes, or having an extra person attend as notetaker, Fireflies saves time and effort by recording and transcribing your meeting providing you with summary notes and actions within a few minutes.

There's so much more to Fireflies than automated note taking. Other use cases include:

- **Organisational listening/focus groups**

Fireflies means you don't need to split your attention between facilitating focus groups and note taking. You can also quickly find quotes, identify themes and AskFred can help with writing up reports with key findings and recommendations.

- **Content creation**

You can use the AskFred feature to perform follow-up tasks such as writing emails and blog posts. Asking questions about what happened during the meeting makes it easier to identify themes and insights for report writing.

- **Creating transcripts from podcasts or Town Hall meetings**

The ability to upload MP3 and MP4 means you can transcribe audio content created outside Fireflies quickly giving you a low cost way to make your content inclusive and accessible.

- **Improving team meetings**

Fireflies can identify who is speaking, the level of contribution from each participant, tone, and sentiment in the conversations. You can use this insight to uncover how your team interacts, who is driving conversations, and the overall sentiment in discussions. Future meetings can be structured to optimise teamwork, productivity, and engagement among members.

- **Streamlining CRM**

Fireflies integrates with workflow tools such as Asana, Monday.com and Salesforce making it easy to send meeting notes directly to your CRM system.

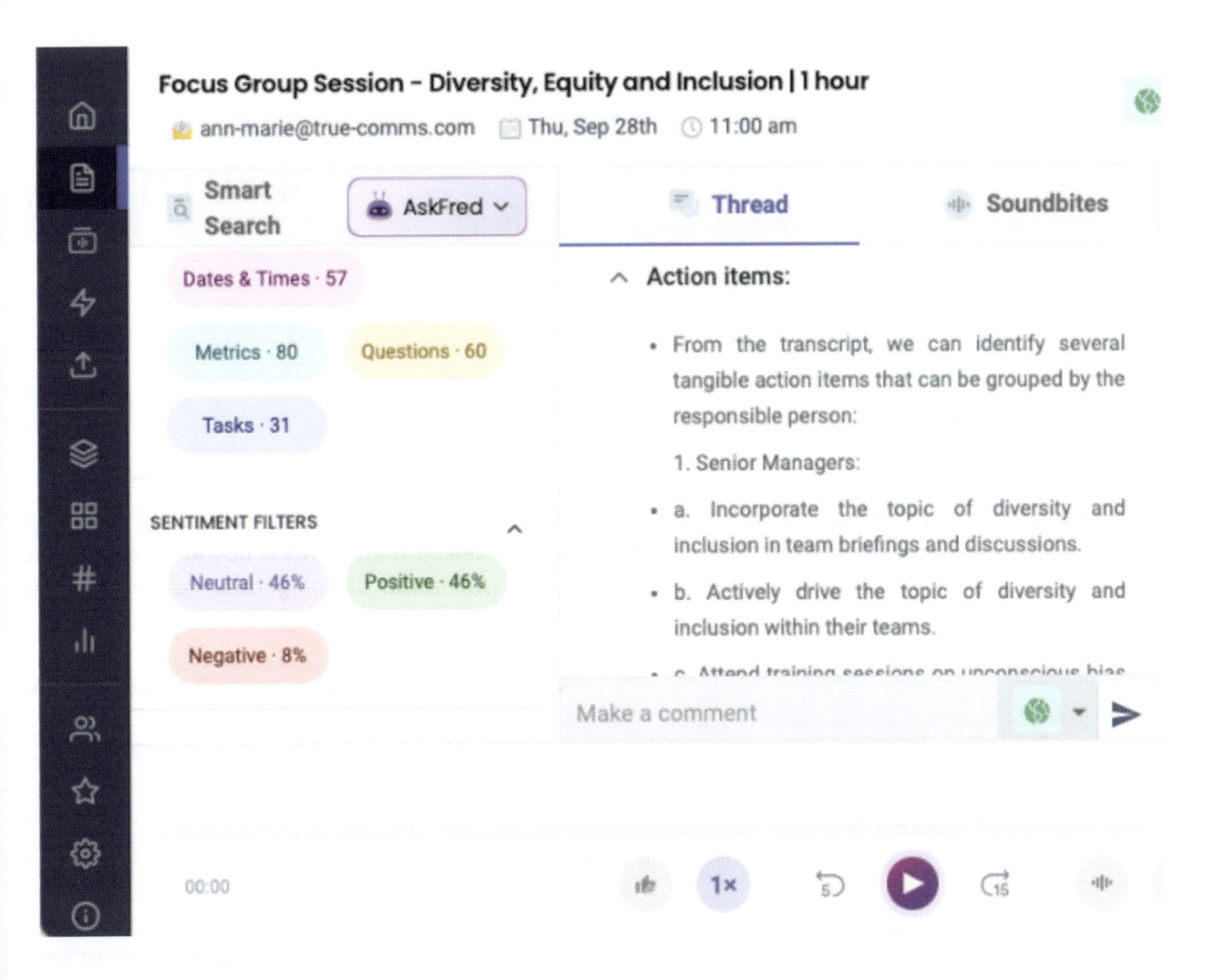

Downsides

The app joins as an added attendee, requiring manual admittance to some meetings. For online training sessions, attendees receiving full transcripts could potentially reveal intellectual property.

Overall, Fireflies delivers tremendous opportunity to enhance productivity, collaboration, and insights.

Ann-Marie Blake, co-founder, True
https://www.linkedin.com/in/ann-marie-blake/

Ann-Marie Blake is co-founder of True, a strategic communications agency. She is on the Executive Board of the IABC (International Association of Business Communicators) and founder member of PRCA Race Ethnicity and Equity Board.

#FuturePRoof: Edition Six

CHAPTER
08

CHAPTER **08**

OTTER.AI

Tom Beswick | Practitioner

Otter.ai is an AI-powered transcription tool that streamlines content gathering, meeting minute taking, and media monitoring for public relations teams by automatically converting audio into editable text.

A lot of AI tools have launched to market in the last 12 months, and it is easy to forget some of the services that have been around for several years.

Otter.ai is one of those tools. And yet, despite the growing collection at our fingertips, this innovative automated transcription and voice note service remains one of the most useful, demonstrating its value across multiple industries, of which public relations is one.

Part of the role that comes with being a public relations practitioner requires talking to people, whether that is journalists, clients, agencies, or consumers. Over the last 100 years, those conversations have been relayed by shorthand and voice dictators, all before the arduous and time-consuming task of transcribing would need to be completed.

Otter.ai removes all of that and has become an invaluable part of a practitioner's arsenal when it comes to improving both the accuracy and efficiency of audio transcription.

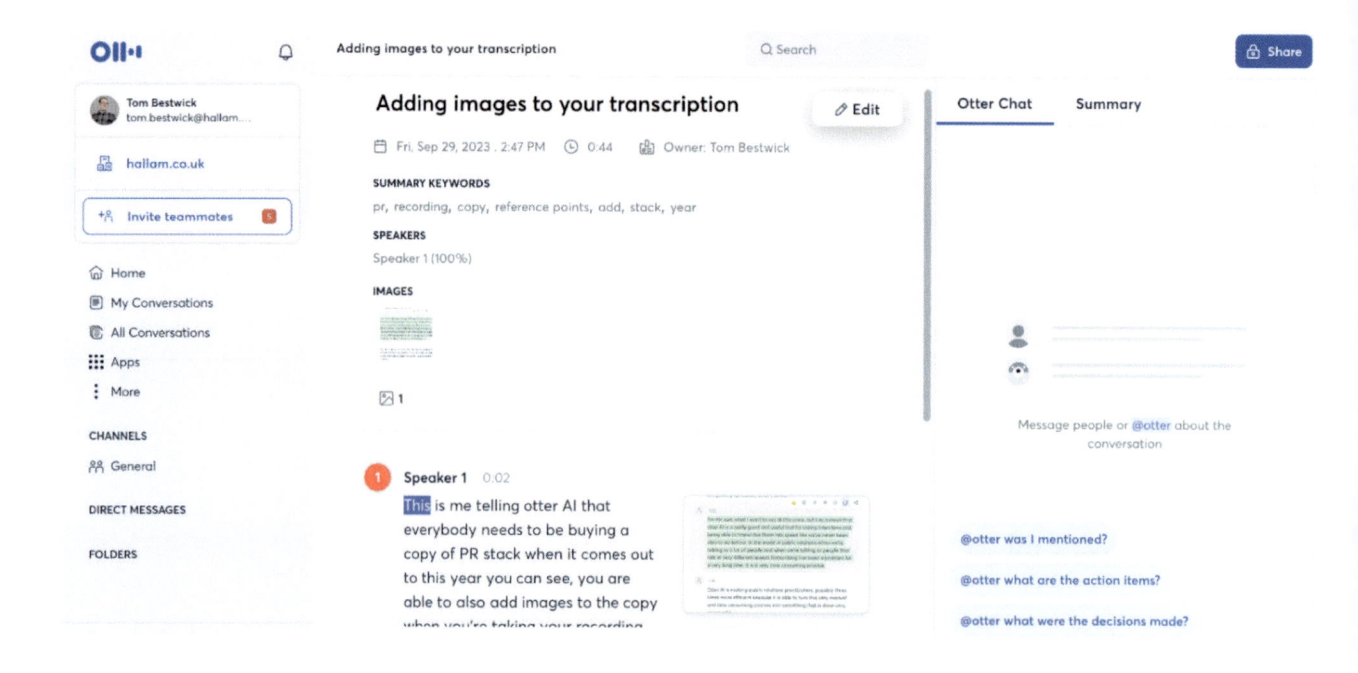

What is Otter.ai?

While Otter.ai is an automatic transcription and voice note service powered by artificial intelligence at its core, in 2022, the service added a series of new features for Business and Enterprise users, making it a one-stop-shop for meeting management - aided by its capability to connect with our essential daily management and communications apps including Slack, Zoom, Dropbox, and both Google and Microsoft Calendar.

Otter.ai has sophisticated algorithms that can accurately transcribe spoken words into written text in real-time. Since launching in 2016, it has acted as a personal assistant - now known as an OtterPilot - that records meetings, interviews, and brainstorming sessions, all while removing the time-draining process that comes with transcribing.

Data shows that, on average, it will take a human as long as four hours to transcribe a one-hour-long audio file. Tools such as Otter.ai complete this task in a matter of seconds, freeing our hands up to focus on the final edit and putting the copy to good use.

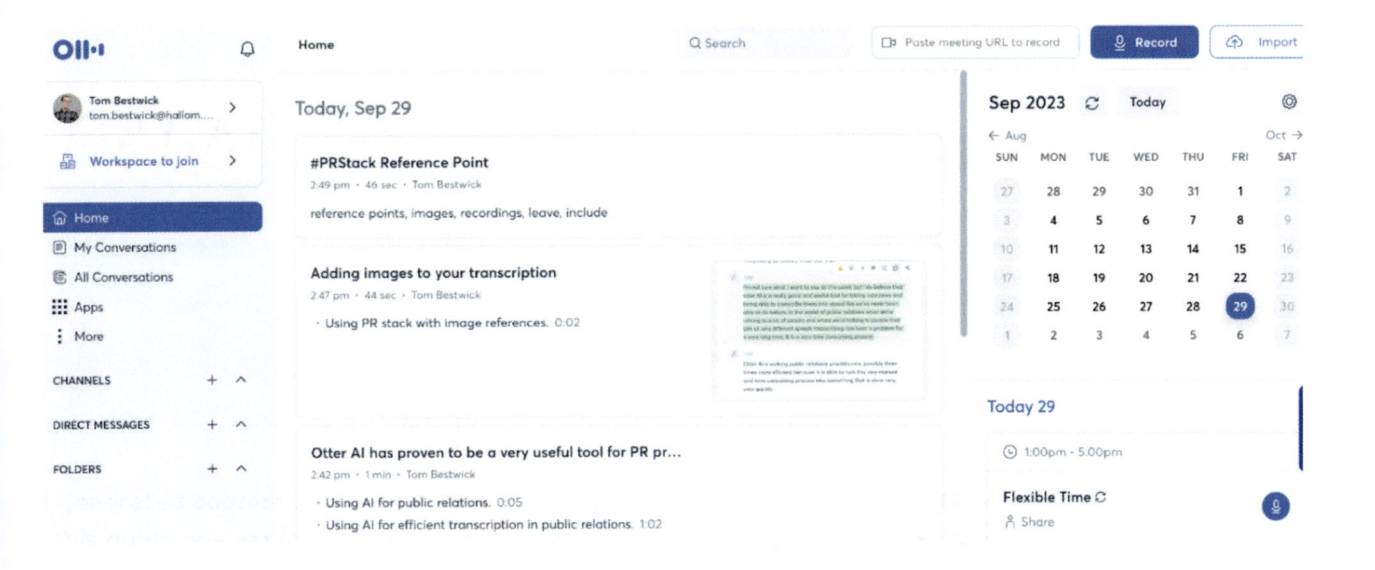

Where Otter.ai fits within the public relations workflow

Otter.ai mostly operates at the content-gathering stage of the public relations workflow.

In the example of public relations, let's say there has been some national breaking news that you feel one of your clients is well-placed to add commentary to. Time is of the essence and by recording a short interview with your stakeholder and gathering their insights and expertise, you can quickly package up their thoughts and respond to the opportunity as quickly as possible but also repurpose the commentary for other communication tools.

This is just one example of how Otter.ai is making public relations practitioners more efficient while making tactics such as reactive public relations more competitive. Other uses of AI include meeting minutes, content creation and media monitoring.

Meeting minutes

During client meetings or internal brainstorming sessions, Otter.ai can record and transcribe discussions, eliminating the need for manual note-taking and allowing public relations practitioners to actively participate in the conversation and demonstrate creativity unhindered.

1:02

I'm not sure what I want to say at this point, but I do believe that otter AI is a really good and useful tool for taking interviews and being able to transcribe them into speed like we've never been able to do before. In the world of public relations when we're talking to a lot of people and when we're talking to people that talk at very different speeds transcribing has been a problem for a very long time. It is a very time consuming process.

1:35

Otter AI is making public relations practitioners, possibly three times more efficient because it is able to turn this very manual and time consuming process into something that is done very, very quickly.

Content creation

Tying into the first point, Otter.ai expedites the content creation process. A focused 30-minute conversation with an industry expert will yield a range of content opportunities that can be utilised across press releases, blog posts, and social media. Otter.ai saves time but also ensures the original ideas and thoughts are preserved in the content.

Media monitoring

A core part of the role of public relations practitioner is keeping abreast of the trends for those we represent. With broadcast media, Otter.ai can transcribe content from radio and television broadcasts, podcasts, and online videos. Beyond transcribing it, though, the output provides accurate and searchable content that can be analysed to identify trends, track media mentions, and measure the impact of campaigns.

Tom Bestwick, digital PR lead, Hallam
https://www.linkedin.com/in/tom-bestwick-pr/

Tom is a public relations and communications practitioner with over 10 years of experience. He leads the digital public relations function at Hallam, where he has worked after gaining experience within the football, leisure management and retail sectors.

#FuturePRoof: Edition Six

CHAPTER
09

CHAPTER **09**

OVERTONE

Christopher Brennan | Developer

Overtone leverages AI to provide qualitative analysis of media relations coverage by classifying articles into categories such as quick hit or investigation, giving insight into campaign impact and pitch resonance.

Overtone provides qualitative content analytics. This gives insight to coverage reports, using Large Language Models and Natural Language Processing on the text of articles themselves. The tool classifies coverage into editorial categories: feature, investigations, quick hit, or hot take.

How Overtone fits into public relations workflow

The scores are most useful in evaluating a campaign and planning for future ones. It helps teams access and benchmark the type of coverage that past campaigns have received, to understand what will best suit a client going forward. This information then makes it easier for teams to filter through coverage, without having to sift through coverage to find the articles that are going to be most impactful.

Information is available at the article level but also for individual paragraphs, so that you can also see what sort of statements mention a brand or product. This can be particularly helpful for examining pitch efficacy and seeing what sorts of messages from a pitch resonated and were picked up by journalists, and how those journalists relayed the messages.

How to use it

Content can be ingested by Overtone either via body text or URL, with the articles processed instantly and scores returned on the article and paragraph level. There is an API for integration into other workflows automatically, so that the articles from a campaign can be sent in and article types added to an existing spreadsheet or database. However, the scores are also available through a dashboard that is filterable by topics, dates, types and categories of articles. Charts are also automatically generated to map article types to other goals such as social media reach.

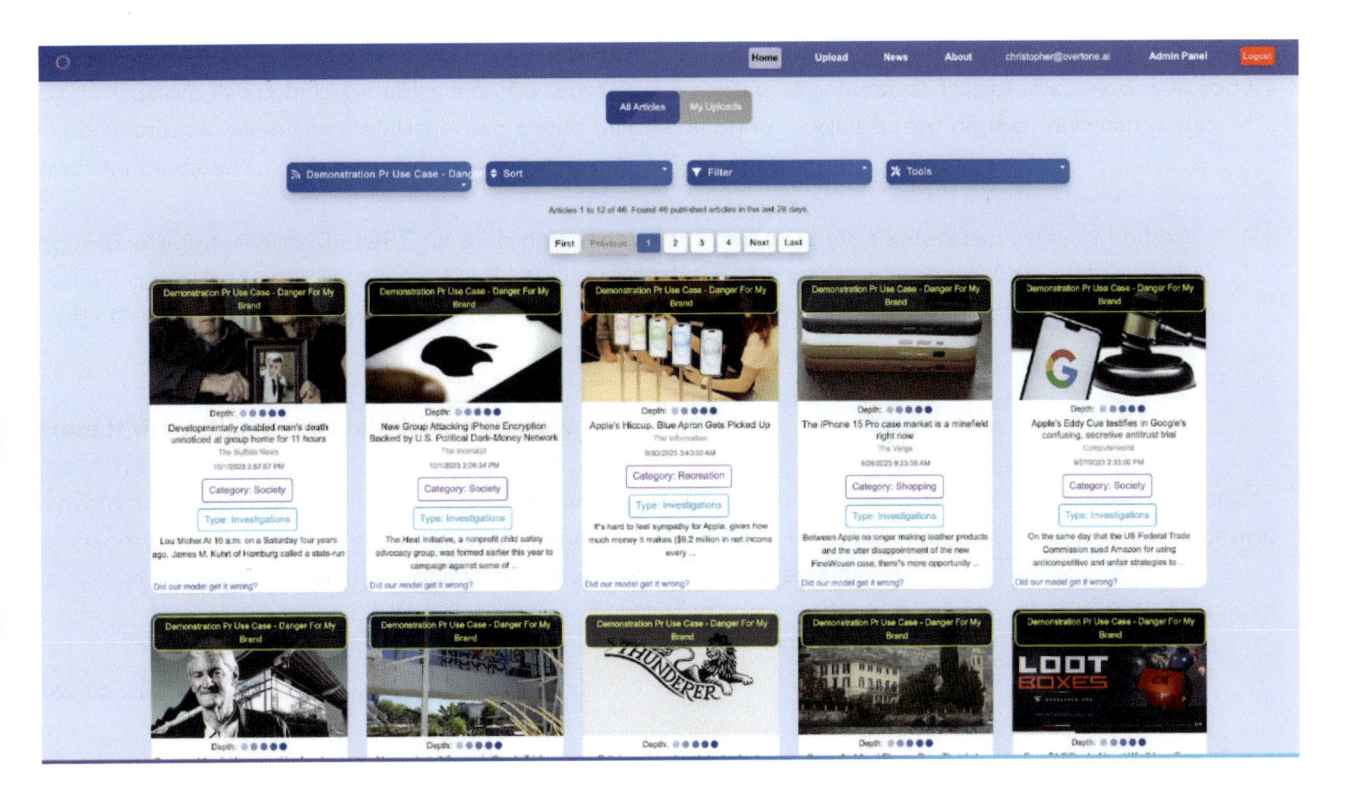

Example use cases

Pitch efficacy

A consumer clothing brand has sent out various press releases over the last several months for different campaigns, with different results in terms of the amount and type of coverage for each campaign. The public relations team is tasked with assessing why the releases led to different coverage.

The team sends articles for three campaigns to Overtone's API to have the content analysed and categorised. They receive the scores and find that for the first campaign, centred on the release of a new headwear product for young adults, more than 70% of the articles written were quick hits about the product release or quick copies of the information in the press release, while 20% were listicles and 10% of the articles were hot takes about the product.

For the second campaign, about the release of a sneaker, more than 80% are Listicles that feature the new sneaker with other products. For the third campaign, about the partnership of the brand with an influencer, the practitioners observes that a quarter of the articles were interviews with the influencer about the brand, which they will want to highlight as proof of their work. An additional quarter of the articles are hot takes about the partnership and the rest of a mix of quick hits and listicles. The AI-generated labels mean that humans do not need to manually label these articles.

Which Types of Article Were Written on my Campaign?

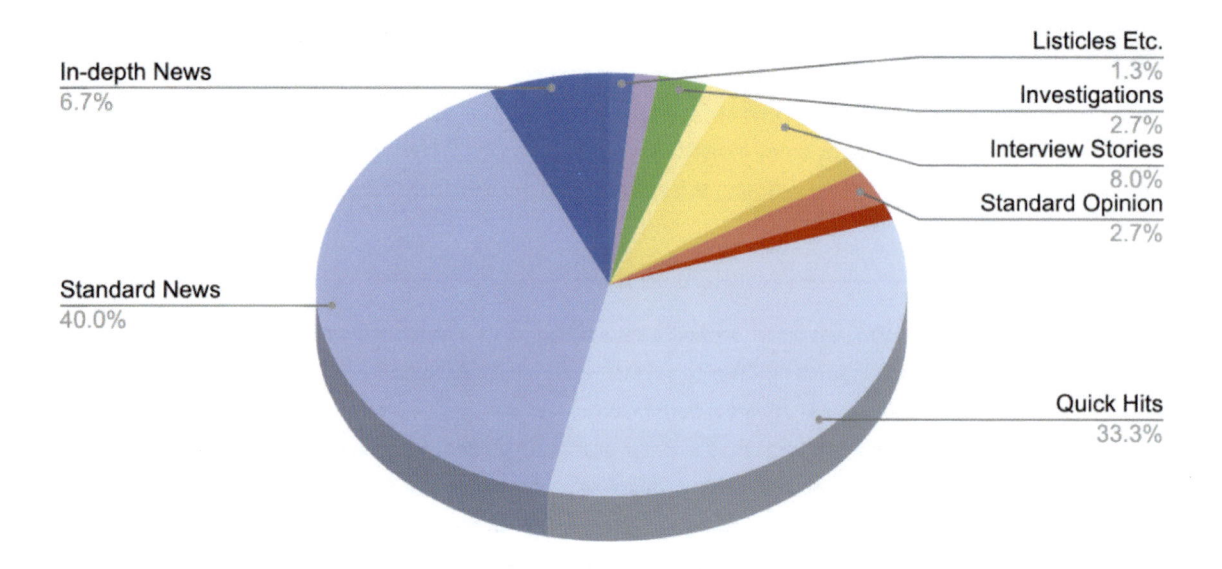

- Listicles Etc. — 1.3%
- In-depth News — 6.7%
- Investigations — 2.7%
- Interview Stories — 8.0%
- Standard Opinion — 2.7%
- Standard News — 40.0%
- Quick Hits — 33.3%

Messages about product

In the previous example, the team wants to do a more fine-grained analysis of the messages from the press releases that were transmitted in the coverage. They send the messages from each release to Overtone, which discovers that messaging about the headwear product was presented in an opinionated way, and that the message was repeated most often in that same opinionated way in hot takes. By contrast, the sneaker messaging was presented in a drier, more factual way, which led to the listicles, with teams able to tailor future releases to lead to the preferred content.

Christopher Brennan, co-founder, Overtone
https://www.linkedin.com/in/christopher-brennan-65565950/

Christopher began his career as a reporter with bylines from a dozen countries for outlets such as the BBC, NYDaily News and France 24. After covering tech he has moved to building it, leading the development of language models for news at Overtone.

#FuturePRoof: Edition Six

CHAPTER
10

CHAPTER **10**

JASPER

Cherise Glymph | Practitioner

Jasper AI is a generative AI writing tool that aids public relations practitioners in quickly creating high-quality, impactful content for campaigns and other communications needs.

Jasper AI is a generative ChatGPT AI-powered language tool that produces impactful, easily digestible, and engaging content for all manners of public relations practitioners. Jasper AI is the premier content curation and creative campaign development tool everyone should use. It doesn't replace human knowledge, understanding, thoughtfulness, or curiosity but augments our ability to create content.

In today's fast-paced media landscape, where social media plays an integral role in news dissemination and brand identity, public relations practitioners are pressured to deliver high-quality content quicker than ever. Tools such as Jasper AI are helping communications practitioners stay ahead of the curve by enhancing campaign and content management. Critically, it helps to get your thoughts down on paper, saving numerous hours and writer's block.

Jasper AI is like a superpower in your pocket or your web browser. It empowers and supports practitioners instead of replacing them. Instead of hours or days, it's ensuring that the first step in creating meaningful content happens quickly and efficiently.

Jasper AI refines initial ideas, guiding creators towards concise, powerful content. It's about delivering solid and meaningful messages in real time. While the platform requires a membership, the Jasper AI Writing Assistant app offers limited free use for tasks like SEO keyword upscaling, content creation, and editing, with an option to upgrade to a premium subscription.

It has more than 50 templates for production, ranging from narrative-building to image generation, social media content development, editing, and translation. This allows users to tailor their work to be brand-reflective, highly relevant, and, most importantly, engaging for the target audience.

Example use case

When creating a narrative for a client offering a niche product, I used industry-specific keywords to generate a story that resonated with the brand's audience and category ownership. The feedback and edits generated by Jasper AI helped me to create a pitch that reflected current trends, interesting data points, and topics discussed by top tier one media.

The example shown below uses Jasper AI to create content about vegetarianism.

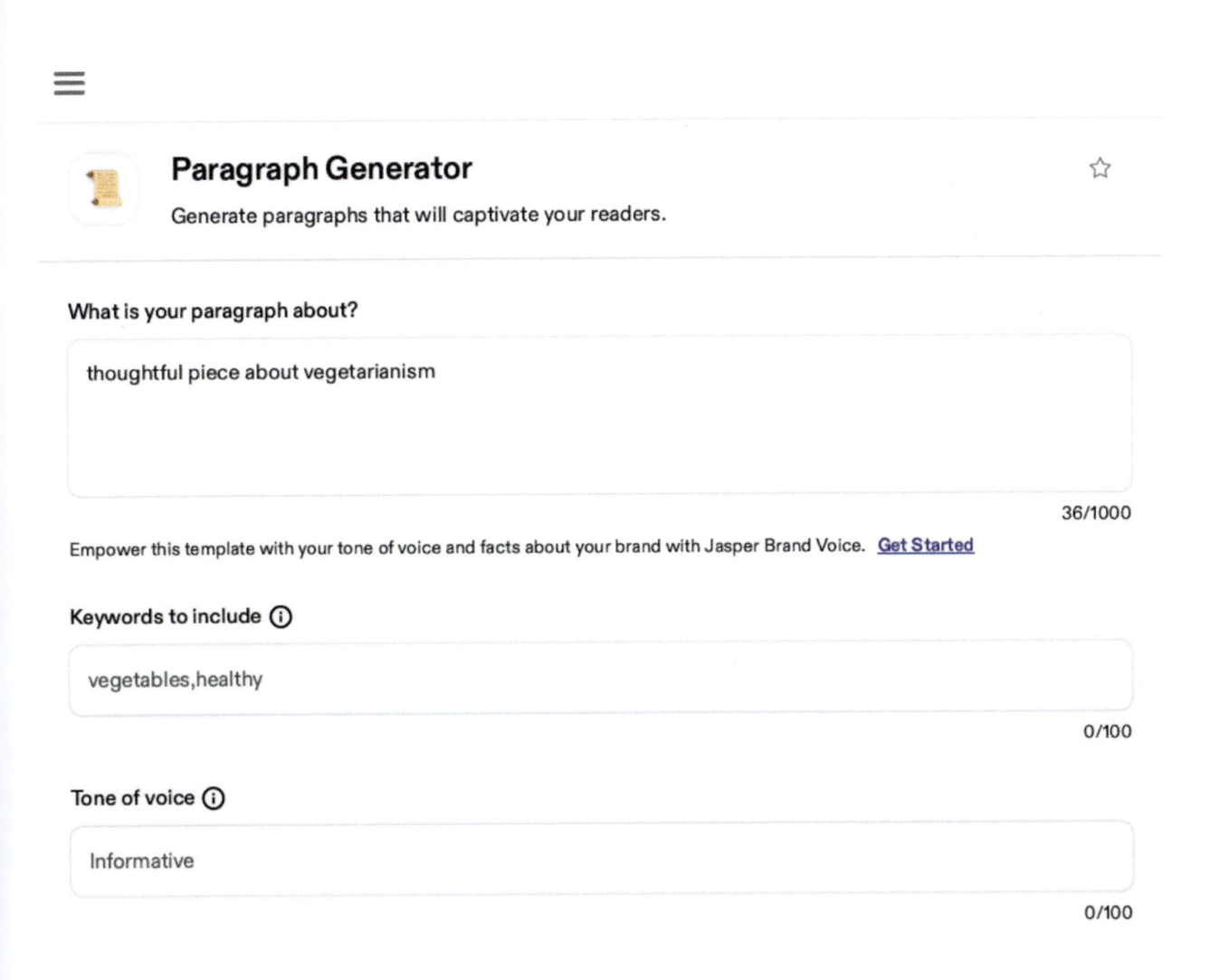

≡

Paragraph Generator
Generate paragraphs that will captivate your readers.

What is your paragraph about?

> thoughtful piece about vegetarianism

36/1000

Empower this template with your tone of voice and facts about your brand with Jasper Brand Voice. **Get Started**

Keywords to include ⓘ

> vegetables,healthy

0/100

Tone of voice ⓘ

> Informative

0/100

> 54s ago
>
> Vegetarianism is a topic that has gained a lot of attention in recent years. The decision to become a vegetarian can come from many different reasons; some choose to do so for health benefits, others for ethical or environmental reasons. But whatever the reason, it is a decision that should be approached thoughtfully. There are many misconceptions about vegetarianism, and it is important to do your research and understand the impacts of your consumption choices. Whether you are a vegetarian or not, taking the time to reflect on your dietary habits can be a valuable exercise in mindful living. By making informed choices about what we consume, we can make a positive impact on our world and the creatures that inhabit it.

> 54s ago
>
> Vegetarianism is more than just a dietary choice, it's a lifestyle that many people have embraced over the years. It's a symbol of compassion towards our animal friends, as well as a conscious effort to preserve our environment and reduce our carbon footprint. Many individuals have chosen to adopt a vegetarian lifestyle for various reasons. Some prefer to abstain from meat purely for ethical reasons, while others do it for health reasons. Whatever the reasons may be, it's undeniable that vegetarianism has gained a lot of popularity in recent times. With the various options available, it has never been easier to embrace vegetarianism and to incorporate it into our daily routines. Ultimately, the decision to become a vegetarian is a personal choice, but one that has benefits for everyone involved.

In addition, the usefulness of their diverse templates and rapid response time allowed me to work on an entire campaign with top-of-mind content for the client. In this respect, Jasper's ability to integrate with other tools is also highly beneficial when working on a multi-faceted campaign.

Jasper AI enables integration with MidJourney, an image-generation tool. This allows users to create visually striking, editorially fine-tuned content – which is incredibly important for communications professionals building visually-led campaigns.

Generative AI tools such as Jasper AI will become essential for campaign work in the future. The tool that can produce the most engaging and relevant content in a user-friendly way.

Cherise Glymph, senior account executive, YourStory

Cherise Glymph began a career in public relations in 2019, working for a boutique technology marcomms and public relations agency called YourStory PR. Prior to this she served as an advocate for a community development agency in Ithaca, New York.

#FuturePRoof: Edition Six

CHAPTER 11

CHAPTER **11**

ANYWORD

Claire Simpson | Practitioner

Anyword is an AI writing assistant that helps public relations teams quickly generate high-performing, on-brand content for different marketing channels while optimising messaging.

Anyword is an AI writer that helps marketers produce more 'on-brand' content. It can generate and optimise copy for marketing channels - including websites, social media, email and ads.

Anyword describes itself as 'built from the ground up for marketers'. It allows users to define their tone of voice, key messages, brand rules, target customer personas and other company details, all in one place.

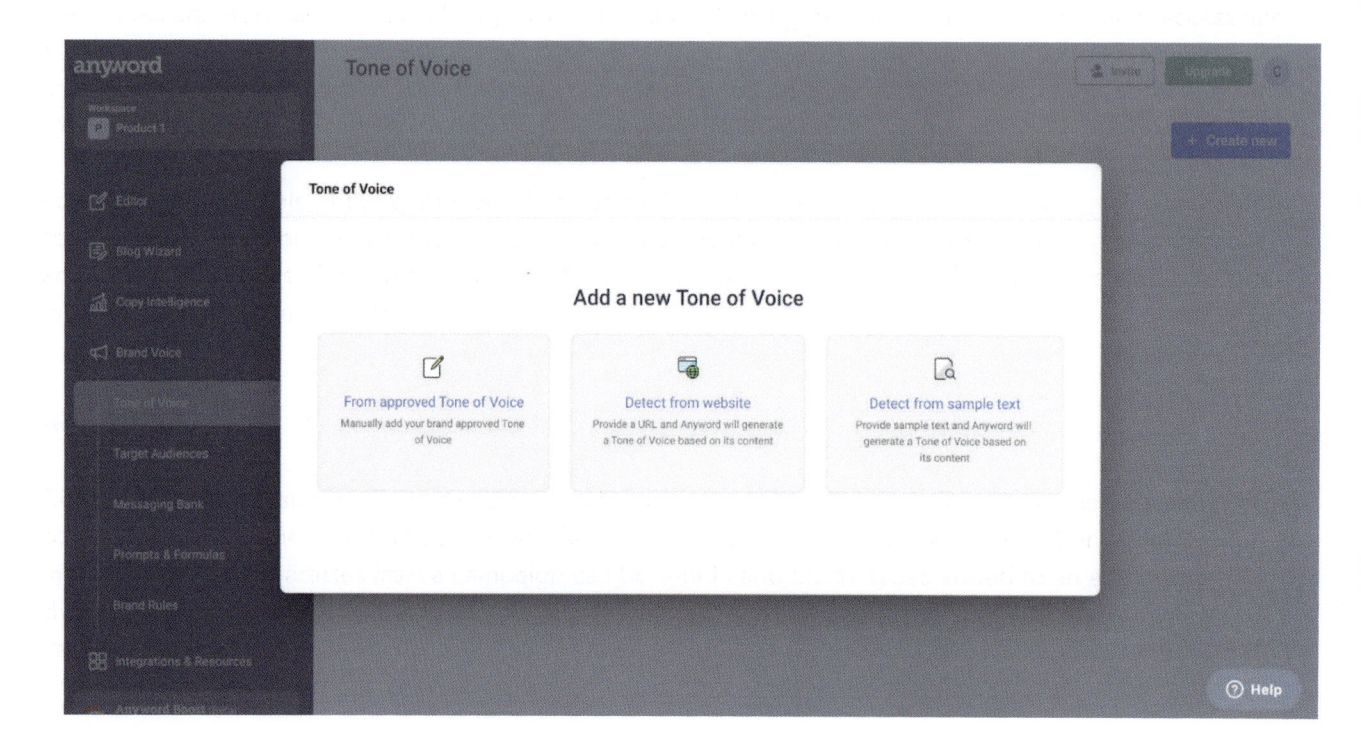

Its 'Copy Intelligence' function analyses content to show what messaging works best on different platforms. And its 'Custom AI Scoring' provides a 0-100 score of the content it generates. This predicts how well copy will perform on a given channel. Users can create tailored scoring models based on their own campaign performance data.

Anyword integrates with ChatGPT via a Chrome Extension. This means marketers can assess whether ChatGPT-generated copy is on brand and how it will perform with target audiences. Other integrations include Canva AI and Notion AI. It is a paid tool with plans starting from $39 per month.

Where it fits within public relations workflow

Anyword augments copywriting and content marketing workstreams. By generating content for core marketing channels and integrated campaigns, it can help amplify public relations activity. Its data-driven editor also supports performance analytics, optimising content to boost conversions.

How to use it

First, sign up for an account at anyword.com. Anyword offers a seven-day free trial across its core plans. Custom pricing is available for enterprise plans.

Next, set up your brand profile under 'Brand Voice'. Here, you can set up a message bank, target audience, tone of voice, brand rules as well as store saved prompts.

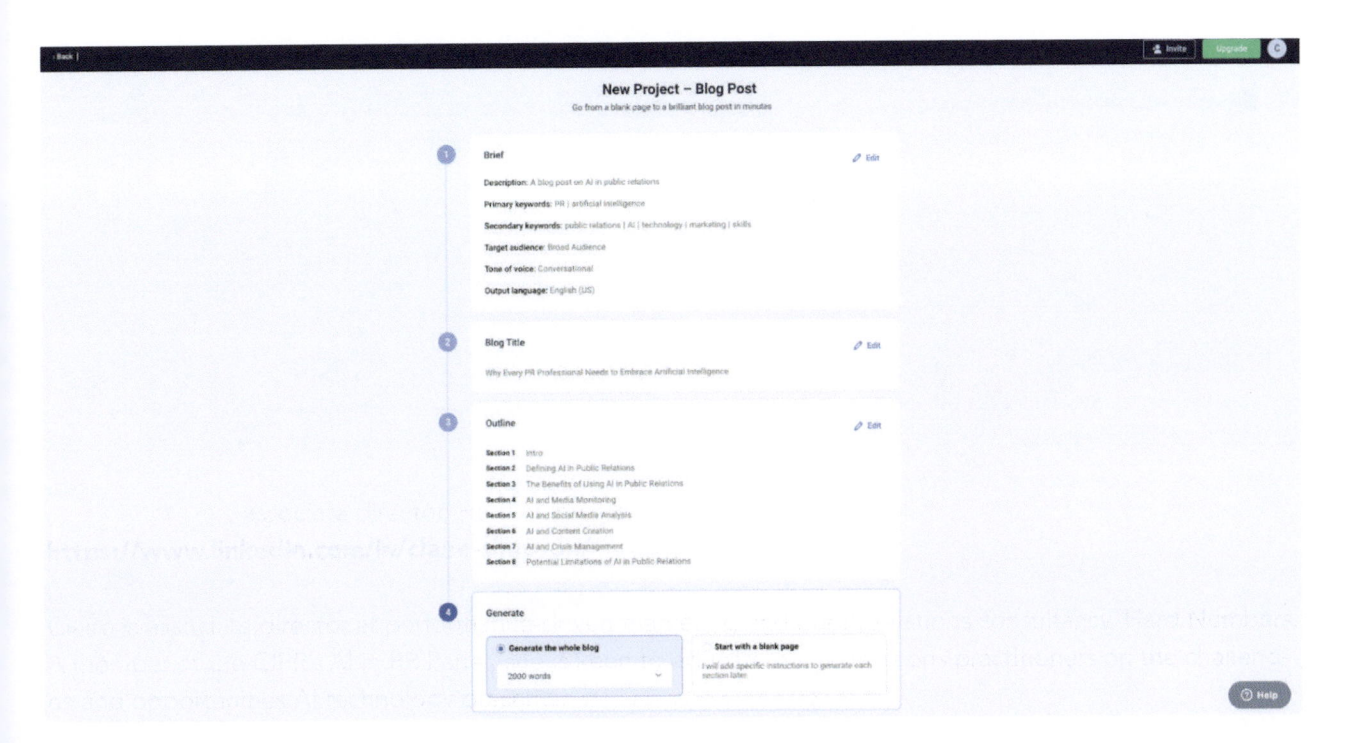

Use the 'Copy Intelligence' feature to audit existing brand content. Review the provided analysis to understand the content that performs best on your channels and inform future output.

Create content using the 'Editor' function. Here, you can select from templates for popular channels, e.g. Instagram captions, Google Ads, landing pages, emails and more. Input details like talking points, target audience and any channel-specific information. Anyword will then generate suggested content, ranked by predicted performance score.

Alternatively, you can use the 'Prompt' function to write any type of content. Or, use the 'Content Improver' tool to optimise existing copy.

For blog content, select the Blog Wizard tool to create a new post. Here, you can provide a summary of the post you want to write, your target audience, tone of voice and keywords. From this, Anyword will automatically generate headline suggestions and a proposed outline. You can then choose to generate the full article or write the post from scratch.

For best results, use Anyword's Custom AI scoring to select the content it predicts will perform best on your chosen channel. If you're an enterprise user, you can train scoring models on your own data. To do this, head to the 'Custom Models' tab under 'Copy Intelligence'.

Example use cases

- **Scaling content production**

Anyword makes it easy to generate content at scale, without losing brand tone of voice. Unlike broad-spectrum AI models, it knows your brand, your audience and what content resonates with them.

- **Optimise conversion rates**

Custom AI content scoring allows you to optimise ad and sales copy to increase conversions.

- **Optimise content for search**

Tailor content to rank for target keywords and drive more organic traffic. Anyword can also identify relevant keywords from existing content.

- **Message analysis**

Review existing marketing materials and content. Anyword identifies which messages work best for different channels and audiences.

Claire Simpson, associate director, Hard Numbers
https://www.linkedin.com/in/claire-simpson/

Claire is associate director at performance-driven marketing and public relations consultancy, Hard Numbers. A member of the CIPR's AI in PR Panel, she is keen to educate public relations practitioners on the challenges and opportunities AI technology presents.

#FuturePRoof: Edition Six

CHAPTER 12

CHAPTER **12**

COPY.AI

Erin Lovett | Practitioner

AI-generated content has been widely adopted by the public relations industry over the past year. In this guide, we explore Copy.ai, a platform boldly promising practitioners the ability to work faster and smarter.

Copy.ai was built to revolutionise the content production process. Leveraging multiple AI models for efficient content creation, the platform prides itself on its adaptability and versatility to draw on the right problem-solving partner for each task. Since launch in 2022 the platform has reportedly amassed more than 10,000,000 regular users, boasting HubSpot, Salesforce and Okta among its customers.

The benefits of AI-generated content are well documented, so I'll spare the details here. For the record – of the platforms I've tried – I would say that Copy.ai boasts one of the simplest and cleanest interfaces, and the ability to browse tried and tested prompts removes the guesswork needed with other platforms. It's a refreshing inclusion which amplifies the platform's desire to improve the efficiency of the end user.

There are two new features which have already added tangible value to the day to day of my role.

Brand Voice

Launched in June, Brand Voice allows copy and content creators to effectively inject their brand's distinctive tone, style, and more to make sure the content generated always aligns with the brand personality, tone and style.

To begin, Copy.ai will ask for copy examples which best represent the brand's unique voice. Once these are fed in, the platform will analyse the copy within minutes or even seconds, offering insight on the tone, how to harness it, and what key messages to land. An unlimited number of brand voices can then be saved, helping you to keep consistent writing across all tasks.

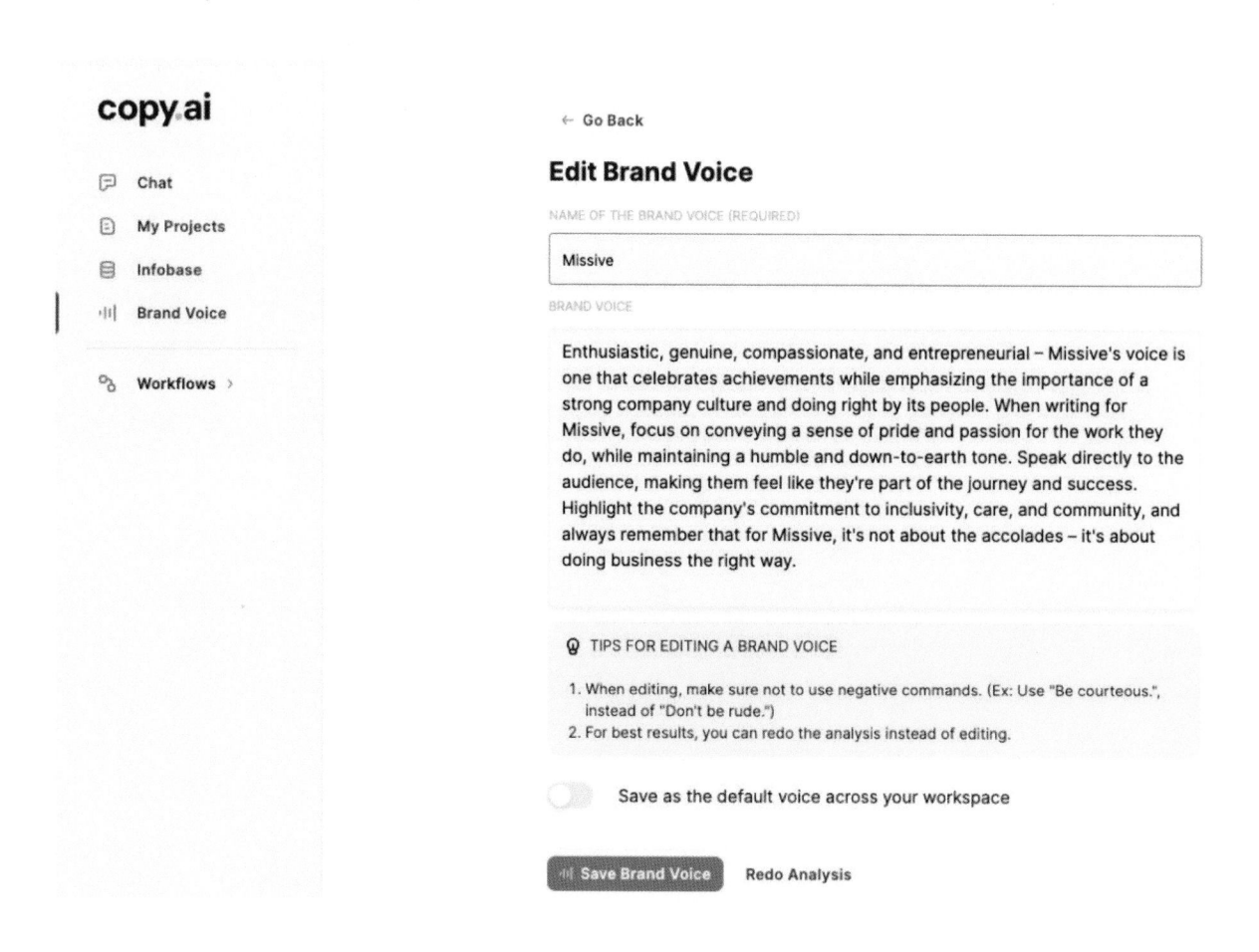

What's unique, however, is the feature can be referenced easily to generate content specific to said brand. It's not only quick, intuitive and accurate, but having a clearly defined tone of voice and style which can be utilised by multiple account team members at any time drives consistency. Couple the Brand Voice with the prompt library, and day-to-day jobs such as creating content calendars or brainstorming SEO keywords can be significantly streamlined.

Infobase

Infobase allows users to store information about their brand that can be referenced and used to improve the quality of content generation.

Whereas other generative AI software may output solid content, it often fails to reference key company information. This feature aims to eliminate that problem and can store everything from brand guidelines to value propositions.

As with Brand Voice, Infobase is protected by its SOC 2 Type II certification, giving peace of mind that Copy.ai provides a safe space for confidential brand information.

The verdict

All content creators know that flitting between different spokespeople and brands multiple times a day can result in muddied and mixed writing styles that lack the intended impact. Copy.ai has gone above and beyond to create genuine efficiencies which its rivalling platforms lack. Both Brand Voice and Infobase eliminate the need for repetitive prompting and are user-friendly innovations capable of becoming useful tools in any creator's arsenal.

What's more (as of October 2023) the full range of features are available free of charge, regardless of which pricing plan you're on. While upgrading to a paid package does result in more seats, languages and output, the free version is generous in its offering.

Like its counterparts, Copy.ai does lack contextual understanding, meaning its output can sometimes be flawed – something which the creators themselves acknowledge. But even so, Copy.ai is a generative-AI tool well worth exploring, blurring the boundary between copywriter and strategic consultant.

Erin Lovett, senior account director, Missive
https://www.linkedin.com/in/erinlovett/

Erin Lovett is a senior account director at Missive, an award-winning integrated public relations communications specialised in technology. She currently leads the agency's content marketing and creative arm and specialises in driving fintech growth across the business.

#FuturePRoof: Edition Six

CHAPTER 13

CHAPTER **13**

WORDTUNE

Ali Yaseen | Practitioner

Wordtune is like having a personal assistant whose job it is to polish your words and make you more productive while you are writing. It makes it easy for you to create a top-notch piece of writing, no matter if you are writing emails, documents, or even chatting with colleagues.

How Wordtune fits into public relations workflow

I use the tool to help me with many tasks such as:

- Content creation: to edit my press releases, features, emails, pitches, LinkedIn posts, and blog posts
- Summarising long documents: reports, studies, and long form articles

How to use Wordtune

Wordtune is a paid subscription. It offers the user two different services: Write and Paraphrase and Read and Summarise.

With the first tool, Write and Paraphrase, you can generate content with AI, rewrite sentences or paragraphs, use specific tones to fit your messaging, save content to your library, and much more. It helps you find different, creative ways to express yourself at a higher level.

The second tool, Read and Summarise, serves as your personal AI reading assistant, designed to help summarise complex documents and articles quickly and easily, all while highlighting key points for you. It can even summarise YouTube videos for you.

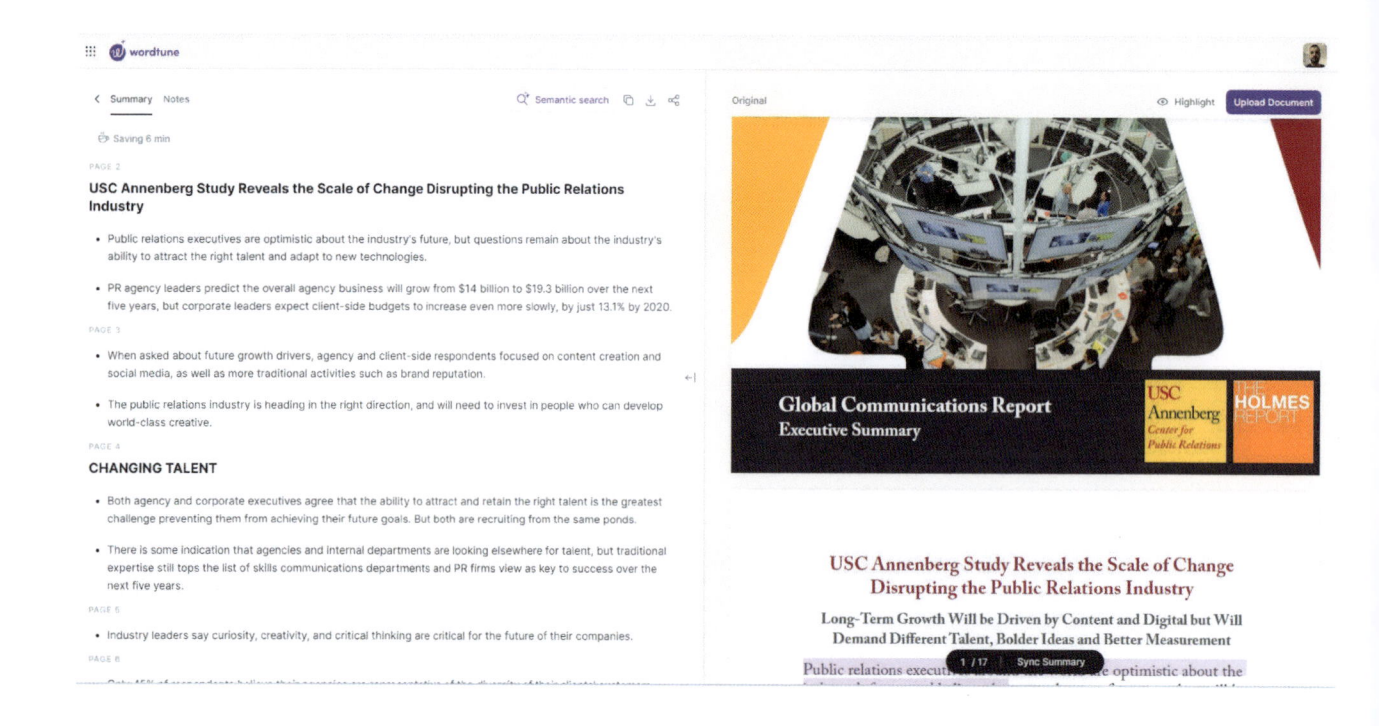

Using Wordtune is as simple as installing the Wordtune Chrome extension on your browser and you are ready to go.

It is possible to activate Wordtune whenever you are writing online by clicking on the Wordtune icon in your browser whenever you are writing online.

Once you have selected the text you wish to edit, Wordtune will immediately offer suggestions and corrections based on the text you have selected. It is, however, important to keep in mind the type of writing style that you want to use. Depending on what type of writer you are, Wordtune can be customised to meet the specific needs of your writing (casual, formal, short form, and long form).

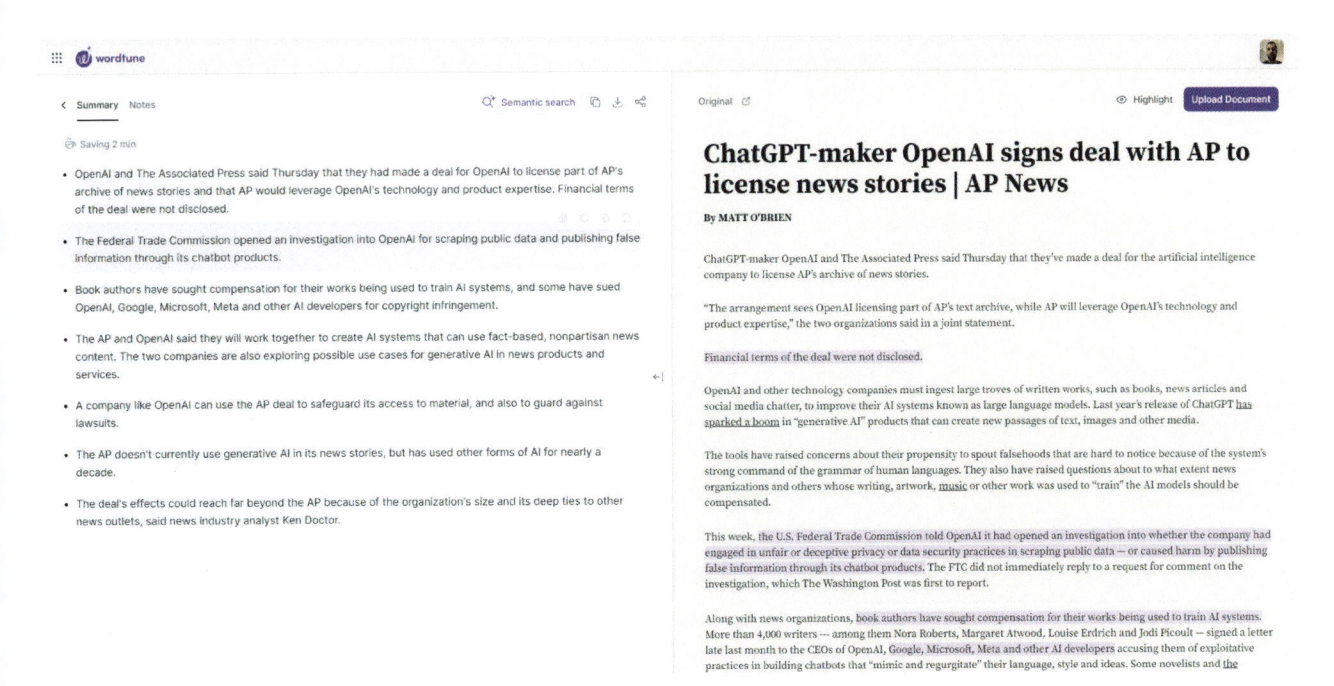

It is also possible to use Wordtune in another way by opening the Wordtune website and placing the entire text you wish to edit there. You will be able to edit this sentence by sentence with the help of Wordtune.

Examples of Wordtune in action

- Press releases: When creating a press release, Wordtune ensures your key messages are clear to understand and free from errors, ensuring your news makes a positive impact on the media by making it interesting to read.
- Emails: When you send out outreach emails, Wordtune helps you to sound professional and error-free, increasing your chances of hearing back from the person you are trying to reach out to.
- Social media posts: With Wordtune, you can make your social media posts more engaging and error-proof, which will boost the online presence of your brand, as well as making your posts more engaging.

Ali Yaseen, associate director, APCO Worldwide
https://www.linkedin.com/in/aliyaseen1304/

A public relations and communication consultant and researcher with ten years of advisory experience across MENA. He leads regional strategy for multinational and local clients across the public, and private sectors, start-up incubators, think tanks, policy research centres, and academic institutions, and help them navigate the complex landscape of modern communication.

#FuturePRoof: Edition Six

CHAPTER
14

CHAPTER **14**

TASKADE

Philippe Borremans | Practitioner

Taskade is a collaboration and workflow management platform that aims to optimise team coordination in public relations by centralising tasks, enabling real-time collaboration, and providing an overview of campaign workflows.

Taskade is a productivity and collaboration platform designed for teams, including those in public relations. It aims to provide a centralised workspace to manage workflows and enhance team coordination.

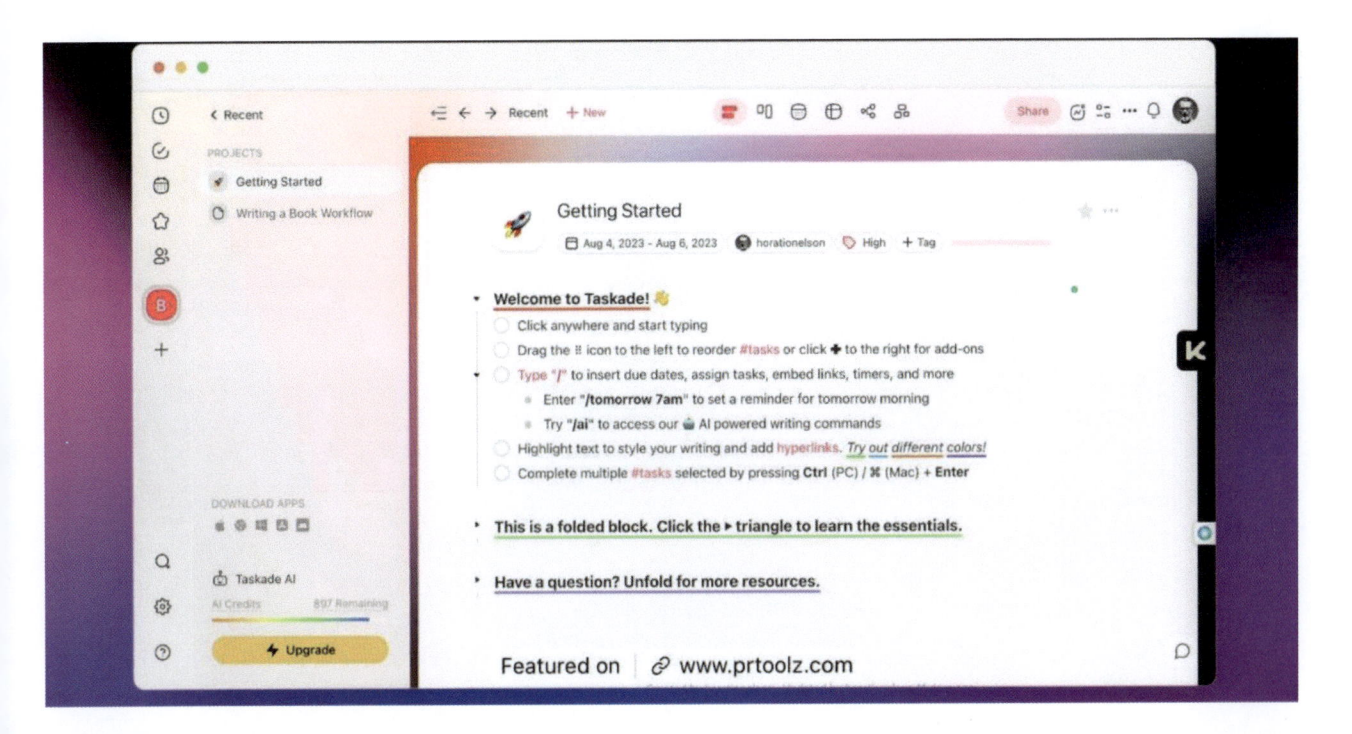

In public relations, professionals often juggle multiple responsibilities simultaneously - media relations, content creation, event planning, reputation management, and more. This leads to managing diverse tasks across different tools and channels. Streamlining collaboration and workflow management are crucial needs for executing campaigns smoothly.

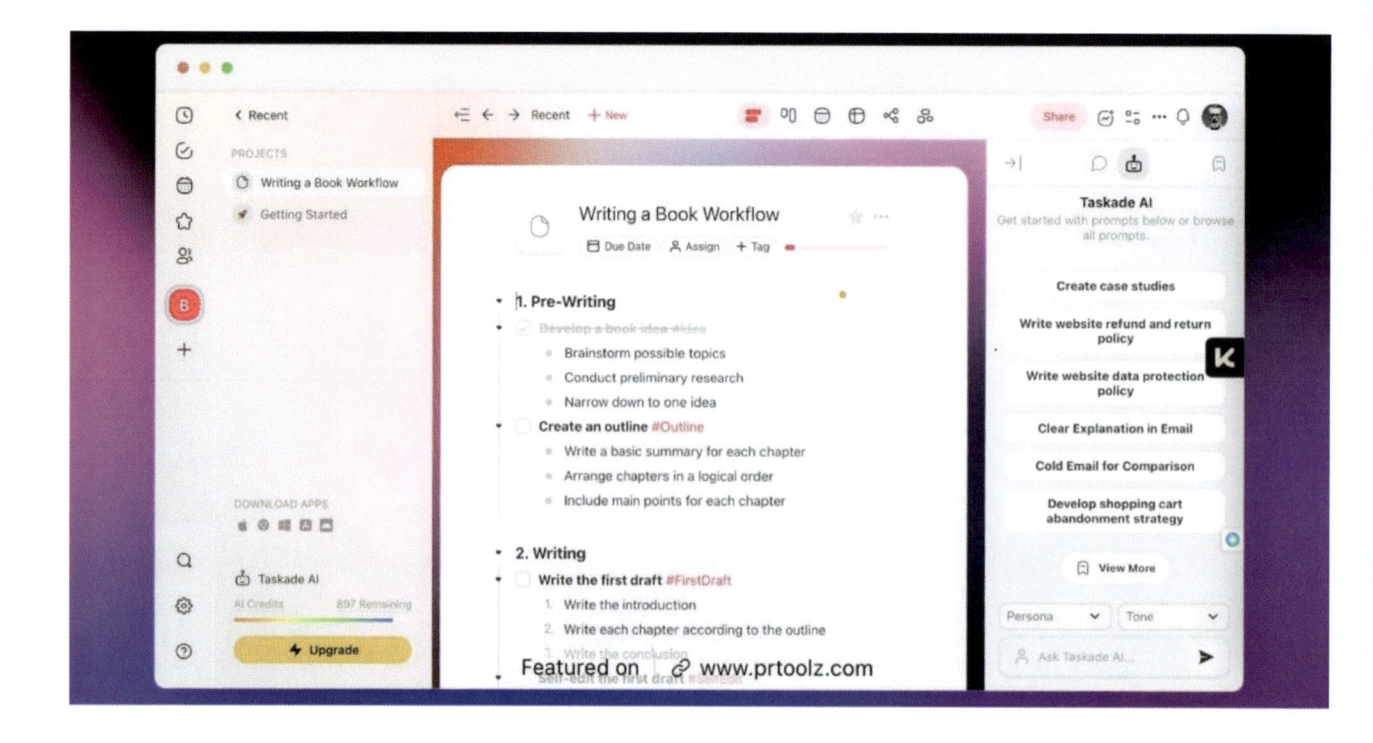

Taskade offers a solution by consolidating tasks into an online productivity platform. At its core, it allows users to create tasks, organise them into projects, collaborate with team members, and track progress on work. However, Taskade goes beyond basic task management through some of its key features:

- **Customisable Boards**

Practitioners can create boards that serve as a shared workspace for each project or campaign. Teams can add task lists, attachments, comments, and more to centralise information on one board.

- **Workflow Mapping**

Taskade enables users to create flowcharts and visualise campaign workflows from end-to-end. Tasks can be assigned steps in the workflow with deadlines.

- **Real-Time Collaboration**

The platform offers capabilities for teams to collaborate in real-time through messaging, video conferencing, and simultaneous document editing.

- **AI Assistant**

Taskade provides an AI assistant to automate certain repetitive tasks like scheduling social media posts, sending reminders, gathering data, and more.

- **Multi-Platform Access**

As a cloud-based tool, Taskade enables access via web, desktop and mobile apps. It also integrates with common tools like G Suite, Dropbox, and more.

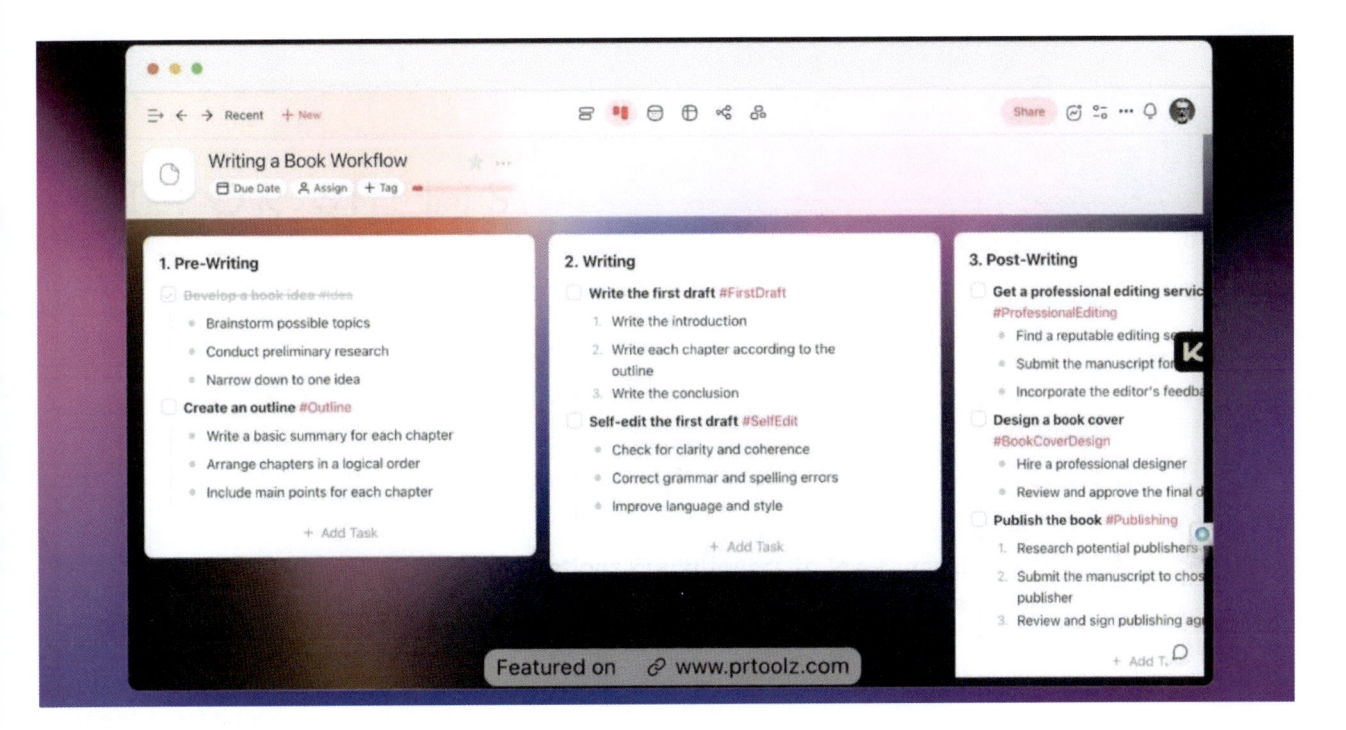

The above features aim to streamline collaboration, provide transparency into campaign workflows, and simplify tasks where possible. This may benefit public relations teams in coordinating seamlessly and improving productivity.

Use cases for Taskade include:

- Planning product launches and tracking rollout tasks.
- Managing social media calendars and scheduling content.
- Overseeing events execution including vendor details and schedules.
- Monitoring issues and crisis communication in a centralised way.
- Maintaining media relations details and coverage reports.

Taskade offers a productivity platform tailored for teams and collaborative work. It aims to be an all-in-one solution for task and project management. The tool consolidates workflows, enables real-time collaboration, and provides workflow visualisation. These capabilities may help streamline coordination for teams across diverse responsibilities.

Philippe Borremans, independent public relations consultant
https://www.linkedin.com/in/philippeborremans

Philippe Borremans is an independent public relations consultant specialising in crisis and risk communications. He is the author of Mastering Crisis Communication with ChatGPT - A Practical Guide and the producer of the Wag The Dog Newsletter and Podcast covering crisis communication and AI.

#FuturePRoof: Edition Six

CHAPTER 15

CHAPTER **15**

GPT FOR SHEETS

Paul Stollery | Practitioner

GPT for Google Sheets enables public relations practitioners to leverage AI to analyse data, reformat content, and automate repetitive tasks, although human oversight is still required.

Building your own AI-driven application sounds like the sort of task that is out of reach for your typical public relations practitioner.

However, thanks to the no code movement, it's easier than you think. If you've got an hour to spare, and you're in the mood to indulge your geekier side, you can start creating custom processes with AI.

This will also give you a greater understanding of the practical possibilities of AI today.

For a layperson, the quickest way to learn about plumbing is to try and replace your bathroom sink. Build something with AI, and you'll immediately be far better at distinguishing between the tangible possibilities of what AI can do today, and the reams of empty promises that are coming out of Silicon Valley.

The easiest place to start is with Google Sheets. You can install an extension called 'GPT for Sheets', and then use GPT to analyse data at scale.

This tutorial will focus on the use cases for 'GPT for Sheets' and how it can fit into the workflow of a public relations practitioner. At the time of writing, instructions on how to install 'GPT for Sheets' can be found here: gpt.space/sheets. If that link is broken, ask ChatGPT.

Use case one: cleaning up your data

Let's say you're running an event and you want to invite marketing practitioners. You've got contacts in your CRM with an email and job title, but no way of filtering by industry.

You can use 'GPT for Sheets' to reference the contact's job title and estimate whether they work in marketing.

1. Download the data from your CRM, and open the spreadsheet in Google Sheets.
2. Use the prompt =gpt("Based on the following job title, does this person work in marketing? Please answer with yes or no.",D2), where 'D2' references the cell with the job title in it.

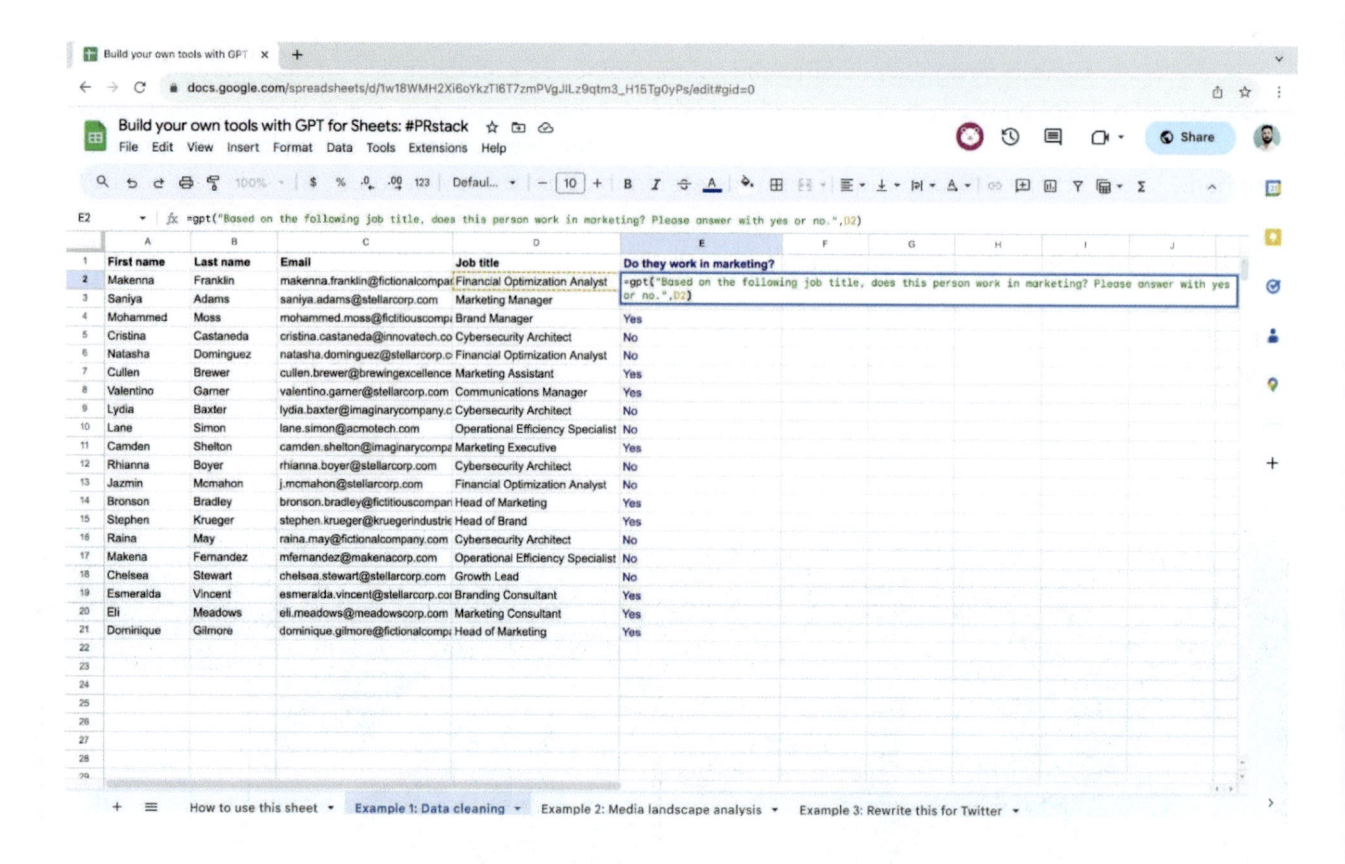

Use case two: media landscape analysis

If you're selling in a funding round for a client, the easiest way to know whether to send it to a journalist is to see if they've written about funding rounds recently.

This is currently a manual process, but if you can get a list of coverage into a spreadsheet, GPT for Sheets can help to automate this process.

1. Download the journalist's details from a media database, and pull a list of their most recent articles into a spreadsheet.
2. Use the prompt =gpt("Based on the following headline, is this article about a technology company fundraising? Please answer with yes or no.",D2), where 'D2' references the cell with the headline in it.
3. Filter by 'Yes'.

Once you've removed the duplicates, you'll have a list of journalists who have recently written about fundraising.

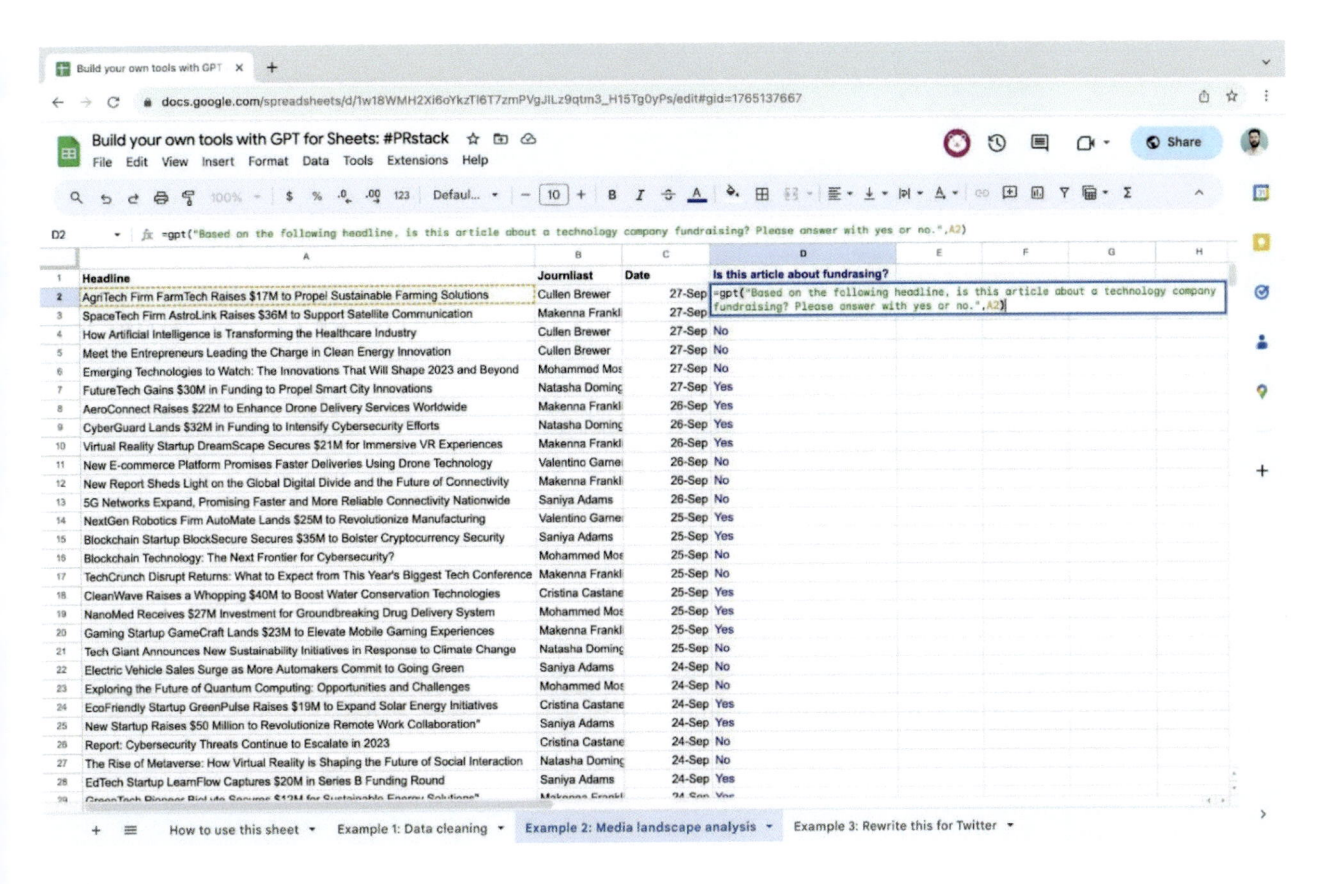

Use case three: reformatting content

ChatGPT isn't great at writing original content. But if all you're doing is reformatting posts, it can produce a solid first draft.

If you've got a content calendar, write the LinkedIn posts first, then ask ChatGPT to provide you with a first draft for other channels:

1. Open up your content calendar in Google Sheets
2. Use the prompt =gpt("Imagine you're a social media copywriter. Please rewrite the following LinkedIn post so it is better suited for Twitter. Keep the style and tone as similar as possible",D2), where 'D2' references the cell with the LinkedIn post in it.

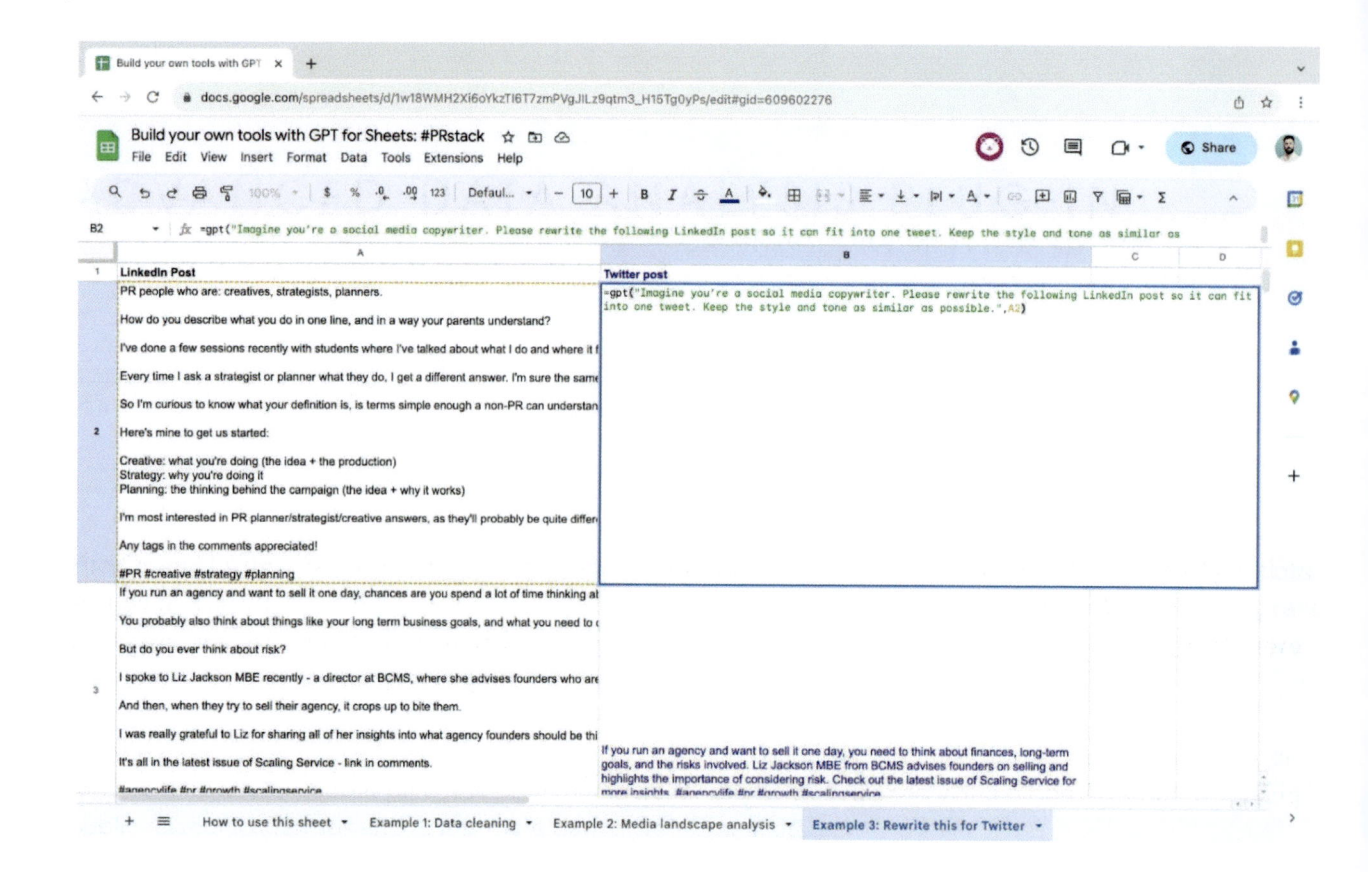

Getting started

For a copy of the spreadsheet used in the screenshots, head to gpt.hardnumbers.co.uk. GPT for Sheets allows you to analyse data and produce content at scale. However, human input is still vital to ensure accuracy and quality. This customisable tool is extremely powerful. Wield it wisely.

Paul Stollery, co-founder and creative director, Hard Numbers
https://www.linkedin.com/in/paulstollery/

Paul is the group creative director and co-founder at Hard Numbers. His role involves overseeing campaign ideation, content creation and managing our network of freelance creatives.

86

#FuturePRoof: Edition Six

CHAPTER
16

CHAPTER **16**

ADVANCED DATA ANALYSIS PLUG-IN

James Crawford | Practitioner

The OpenAI Advanced Data Analysis plug-in allows practitioners without coding skills to analyse data and gain insights by writing in simple English prompts. This feature can help automate tasks like press coverage analysis, audience research, measurement and evaluation, and report generation that were previously time-consuming or required data expertise.

For the past 20 years the public relations industry has seen countless talented account handlers glaze over when faced with talk about purchase order numbers, accounts or data. Sadly, the biggest barrier to making public relations agencies and teams more data driven is data literacy.

The OpenAI Advanced Data Analysis plug-in has changed all that. It has recently been renamed from Code Interpreter. It is still a beta product.

The Advanced Data Analysis plug-in allows users to execute Python code in a sandbox environment. This means that users can write and run Python code without having to install any additional software or libraries.

Most people probably got into public relations for creativity, not coding, but, here's why python code is relevant to practice and can help bring creativity to the fore.

Python code is a set of instructions that tells a computer what to do. It is written in a language that is similar to English, but with stricter rules and syntax. Python code is used for a wide variety of tasks, including data analysis, machine learning, web development, and automation.

The Advanced Data Analysis plug-in allows you to write Python without really knowing the programming language. Not many agencies have access to a data analyst or a programmer who can programme in Python, but now, thanks to the Advanced Data Analysis plug-in they do.

The case uses for the Advanced Data Analysis plug-in are endless, but let's look at it in layman's terms. Imagine an account executive has been asked to look at the brand visibility of a client and has downloaded some search data that shows the branded search volumes per month. The account executive wants to do some simple analysis to look at trends, year-on-year and against seasonality too.

The account executive needs to simplify the data into a CSV and into simple columns with no arbitrary text apart from the titles (the Advanced Data Analysis plug-in currently doesn't like formatting – it just won't work). Then while uploading it the account executive should describe using words what the spreadsheet says when uploading.

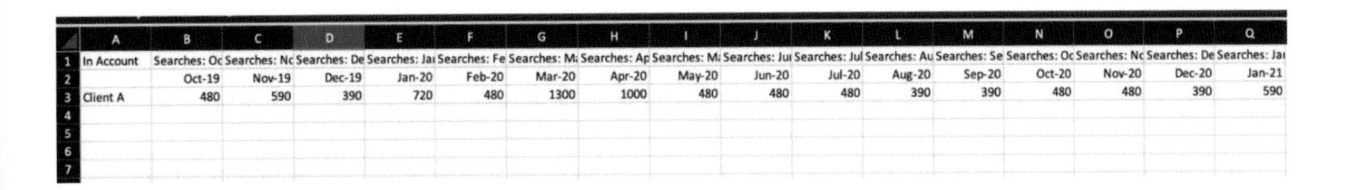

	A	B	C	D	E	F	G	H	I	J	K	L	M	N	O	P	Q
1	In Account	Searches: Oc	Searches: Nc	Searches: De	Searches: Ja	Searches: Fe	Searches: M:	Searches: Ap	Searches: M:	Searches: Ju	Searches: Jul	Searches: Au	Searches: Se	Searches: Oc	Searches: Nc	Searches: De	Searches: Ja
2		Oct-19	Nov-19	Dec-19	Jan-20	Feb-20	Mar-20	Apr-20	May-20	Jun-20	Jul-20	Aug-20	Sep-20	Oct-20	Nov-20	Dec-20	Jan-21
3	Client A	480	590	390	720	480	1300	1000	480	480	480	390	390	480	480	390	590

Once, ChatGPT says it understands the document the account executive can simply ask questions, using very simple language, like ChatGPT is a data analyst.

I first like to start really broad with a question like:

What can you tell me about any trends over time? What can you tell me about seasonality? It first comes back with a description of the data and asks permission to look at it in more detail, to which tell it to proceed.

This is what came back.

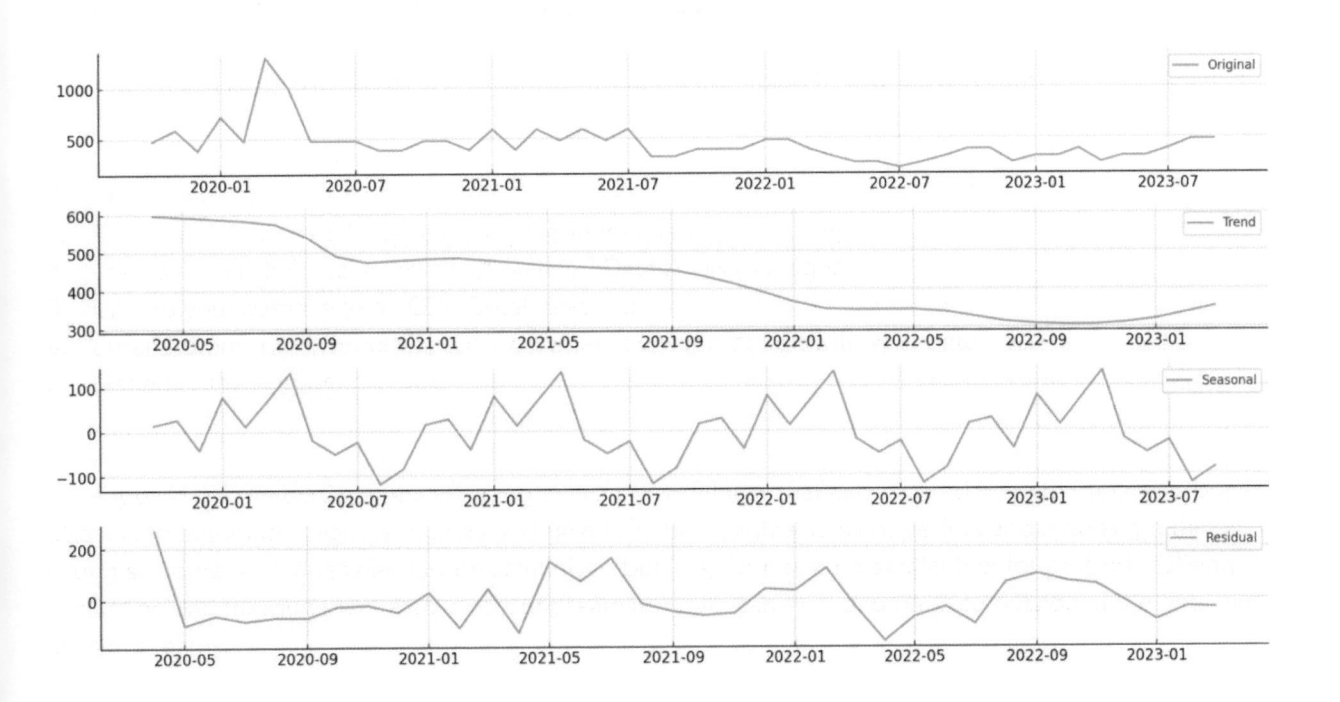

Time-Series Analysis for "Client A"

Observations:

- **Trend:** The trend does indeed show a general decline over time, with a slight uptick in the most recent quarter. This suggests that the branded search traffic for "Client A" has been decreasing but may be showing signs of recovery or stabilisation.

- **Seasonality:** Clear seasonal patterns are observable. Peaks often occur around March and troughs around December.

- **Residuals:** The residuals are the deviations from the trend and seasonal components. These seem random and don't indicate any additional pattern.

Would you like to delve further into any specific aspect?

I then can ask it to look at the last three months in greater detail as this just so happens to correlate with our own public relations activities. We are particularly interested in the year-on-year comparison.

What it comes back with is significantly quicker and better written than most non analysts could do and significantly quicker than even a well paid analyst.

Year-on-Year Comparison for July, August, September

July, August, September 2022:
- Mean branded search traffic: 263.3263.3

July, August, September 2023:
- Mean branded search traffic: 450.0450.0

Analysis:
- Year-on-Year Percentage Increase: There is a 70.8970.89 increase in the mean branded search traffic for July, August, and September 2023 compared to the same months in 2022.

Interpretation:
- The branded search traffic for these specific months has shown a significant year-on-year increase, which aligns well with the broader year-on-year comparison.

Impressive. I can very quickly see the year-on-year increase and describe it to clients professionally.

Other applications in public relations workflow

The example above was deliberately simple but any public relations practitioner with an imagination can now put this tool to good use. Here's a few topline suggestions.

- **Press coverage analysis**
The OpenAI Advanced Data Analysis plug-in can be used to analyse press coverage data from Google Data Sheets that are saved as CSVs. This can help practitioners to identify trends in coverage, identify key influencers, and measure the impact of their campaigns.

- **Audience insights**
It can be used to gain insights into target audiences by analysing data from GWI Index, Google Analytics, keyword data, and SEMrush. This information can be used to develop more targeted and effective public relations campaigns.

- **Measurement and evaluation**
The Advanced Data Analysis plug-in can be used to measure and evaluate the results of public relations campaigns by analysing data from Google Analytics, keyword data, and other sources. This information can be used to identify what is working well and what needs to be improved.

- **Research summaries and insights**
It can be used to generate summaries and insights from public relations research data. This can help practitioners to save time and produce more effective reports.

How to use the OpenAI Advanced Data Analysis plug-in

Getting started is simple. To use the Advanced Data Analysis plug-in you will need to:

1. Create a ChatGPT account.
2. Upgrade to ChatGPT Plus.
3. Enable the Advanced Data Analysis plug-in feature in your settings.
4. Create a new chat and select the Advanced Data Analysis plug-in .
5. Upload your data file (e.g., CSV, Excel, text file).
6. Enter a prompt to instruct ChatGPT on what you want it to do with your data.
7. Generate the output.

The OpenAI Advanced Data Analysis plug-in is a powerful tool that can be used by public relations practitioners to automate a variety of tasks and gain valuable insights. It is not perfect and it does get things wrong so some work does need to be scrutinised but it is, for me, an essential tool for professionalising evaluation and measurement across account teams so data can exist and be used outside of the data and analytics teams.

James Crawford, managing director, PR Agency One
https://www.linkedin.com/in/jameswdcrawford/

James founded PR Agency One, which since its launch in 2012 has put creativity and data at the heart of what it does. PR Agency One's proprietary evaluation system OneEval predates the AMEC framework and has since been developed into three distinct products that focus on three areas Commercial, Reputation and Brand.

(iii)

INTEGRATED AI IN PUBLIC RELATIONS PLATFORMS

#FuturePRoof: Edition Six

CHAPTER 17

CHAPTER **17**

BUZZSUMO

Louise Linehan | Developer

BuzzSumo is trusted by thousands of public relations practitioners, journalists, and marketers across the globe. With the world's largest database of web content and social engagement data, it supports users in analysing trends, reporting on performance, and executing an AI-assisted media strategy.

Where it fits within the public relations workflow

From creating campaign ideas to monitoring media coverage, BuzzSumo helps digital practitioners navigate every stage of their public relations strategy.

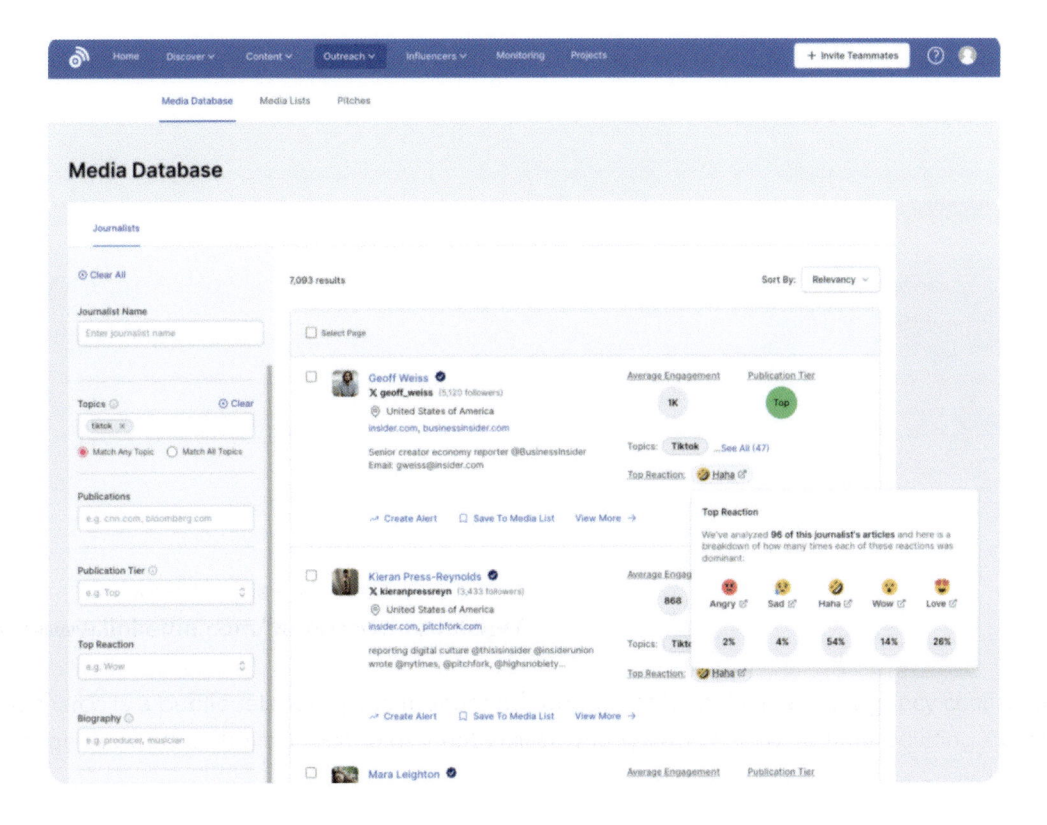

At the time of writing, it uses AI to identify 700,000+ journalists online across publications and social media.

The result is a media database that enables public relations practitioners to tackle some of the biggest problems they face, day-in-day-out:

- Discovering relevant and niche journalists – BuzzSumo combines AI with human-led verification, to discover real journalists writing across thousands of beats and publications.
- Keeping up with personnel changes across publications, and finding active journalists with open inboxes – journalists move around, and editorial teams are leaner than they have been in years. BuzzSumo uses machine learning and AI to push through 300K+ updates to journalist profiles, to arm practitioners with fresh and accurate information on who is writing, what they're writing about, how often they're writing, their most popular articles, and where they're publishing right now.
- Developing ongoing relationships that work for both public relations practitioners and journalists – by linking content and engagement data to AI-discovered journalists, BuzzSumo helps practitioners to: pinpoint the most engaging topics that will drive strong coverage, discover the most engaging journalists to push their story forward, and even help journalists hit their own KPIs. The result is a symbiotic relationship, and ongoing coverage.

AI-discovered journalists

BuzzSumo's AI powered Media Database helps practitioners track down a journalist's contact information, but also gives them visibility over their content archives and engagement over the years.

With this information they can do powerful things; from hyper-personalising outreach, to selectively pitching only the most engaging reporters and publications.

The database also enables users to discover journalists by name, topics, verticals, media outlets, and filter searches by publication date to connect with reporters actively creating relevant content.

Once users identify promising journalists, they can analyse their beat, publication domain authority, content reactions, and engagement metrics.

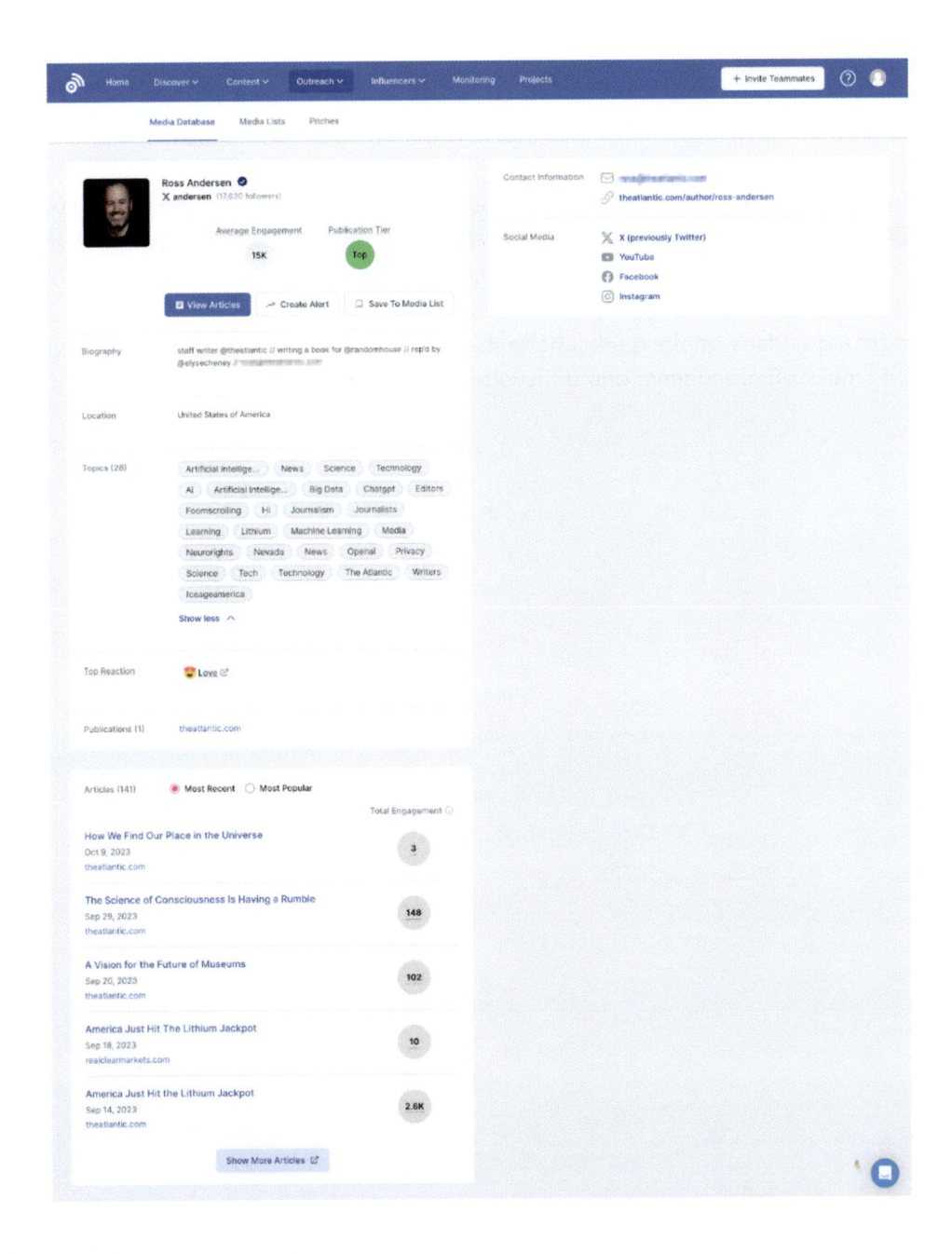

BuzzSumo enables practitioners to bank their AI-discovered journalists to custom media lists for simplified outreach. In this part of the platform they can also:

- Analyse the content of journalists in their list (including engagement, publishing patterns, engagement trends, typical word counts, top content formats/types, average links, evergreen scores, etc.) by hitting an "Open in Content Analyzer" button
- Set up content alerts for specific journalists
- Export their media lists for further analysis
- Pitch their media list

AI-assisted pitching

BuzzSumo also uses generative AI to support digital practitioners in their outreach.

BuzzSumo AI Pitches drafts emails in seconds, so that they can save time drafting copy and dedicate more time to personalisation.

After entering a short prompt describing their campaign's key information and takeaways, practitioners are met with a fully formed pitch generated by AI. They can hit "Regenerate Pitch" for new copy options, and customise until they've crafted their perfect pitch.

AI pitches can be formatted for readability, including bullet points and headings, and practitioners can paste URLs over existing copy to incorporate hyperlinks. They can also adjust the tone of a pitch to better reflect their own style of pitching – whether that be friendly or urgent.

But AI can only go so far – and there's plenty of space for practitioners to add that personal touch. BuzzSumo provides fully populated journalist cards to the left of each pitch, to help practitioners quickly and easily hyper-personalise their emails to the individual journalist.

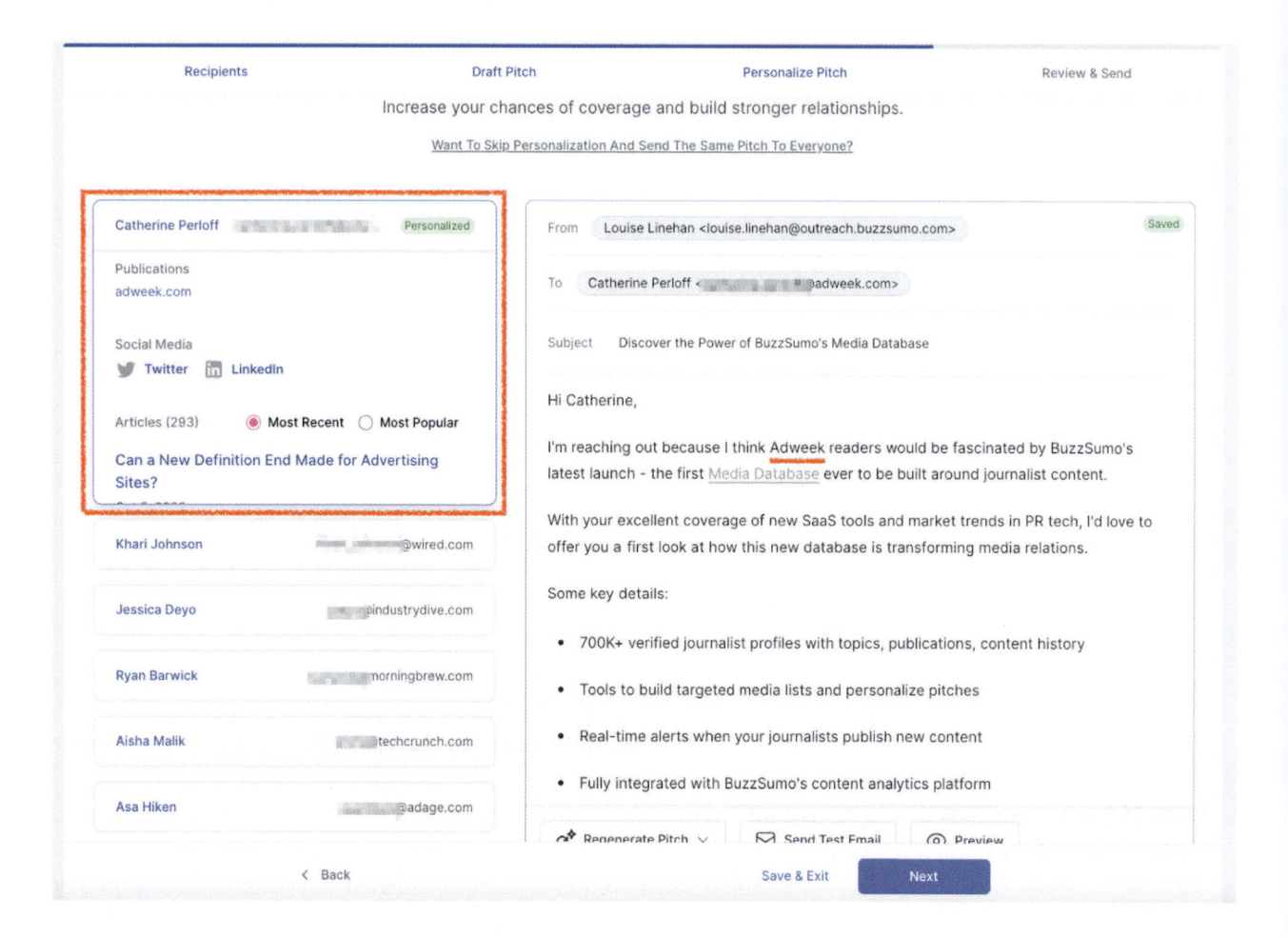

These cards showcase the journalist's latest impactful coverage, social media presence, biographical details, and more – just when practitioners need it most. Reviewing a journalist's own content helps practitioners craft subject lines that spark instant recognition and response.

They can simply review the information on the left and input their personalisation on the right.
Once they're happy with their pitches, BuzzSumo enables users to send and report on their outreach performance in-app, including opens, forwards, and response rates.

And finally, to analyse the impact of their AI-driven outreach efforts, the platform enables practitioners to monitor backlinks to their campaign pages, and discover relevant brand mentions in BuzzSumo Monitoring & Alerts:

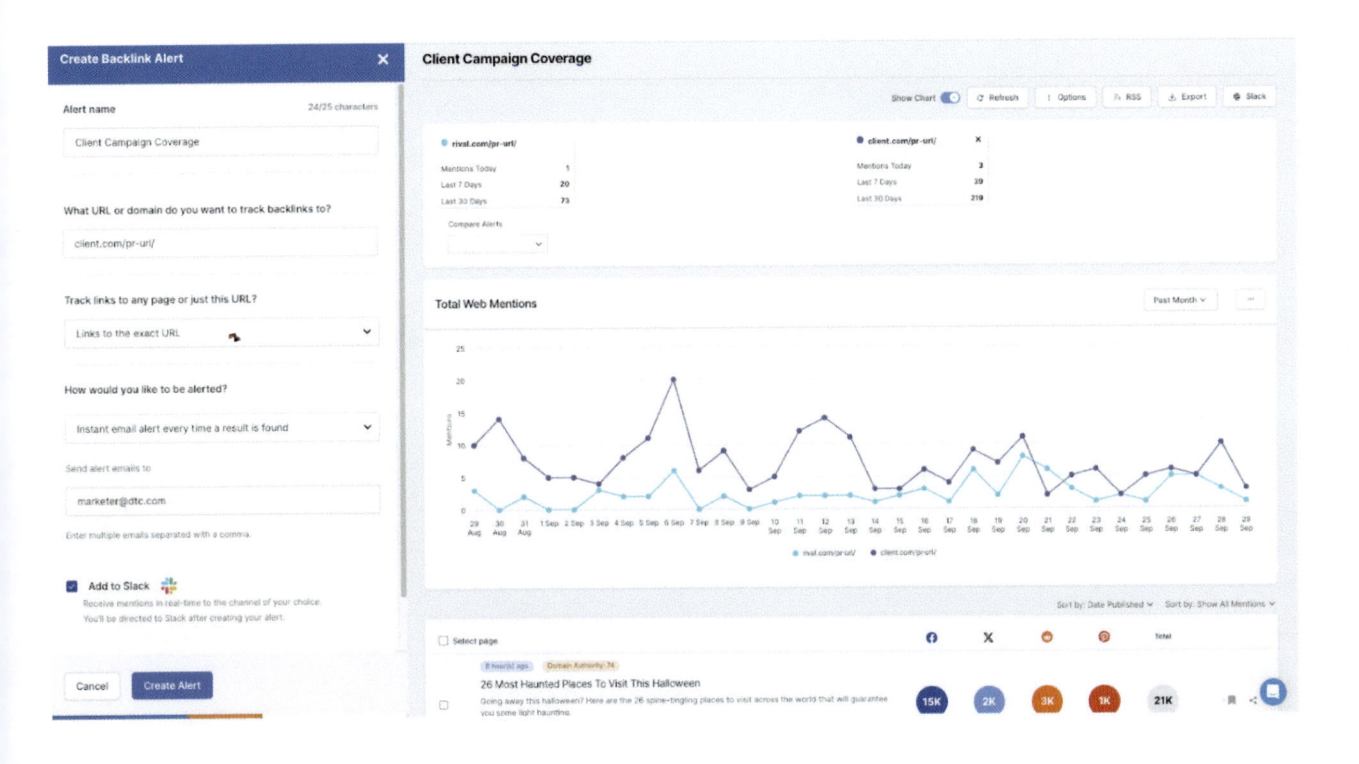

Use case

Agency based practitioners are often tasked, by clients, to win coverage in a specific publication.

Using BuzzSumo's AI augmented toolset, they can not only discover journalists writing for said publications, but also research and analyse the most engaging content on that platform.

In doing so, they can personalise their campaigns to specific publications and journalists from the outset, so that their pitch is guaranteed to appeal.

From a list of relevant journalists writing for the desired publication, they can single out and give pitch-priority to the ones that drive the most links, engagement, and authority.

Then, they can analyse the publication and/or journalist's winning content formats and headline types, understand the emotions they tend to stir up in their audiences, and even track trends in their publishing cadence to get an idea of coverage turnaround.

BuzzSumo's AI toolset doesn't just enable practitioners to seamlessly find and contact journalists, it helps them lay the groundwork for far-reaching coverage.

Louise Linehan, senior content manager, BuzzSumo
https://www.linkedin.com/in/louise-linehan-898229102/

Louise is senior content manager at BuzzSumo, and has worked for hyper-growth startups in the B2B SaaS industry for the last eight years. She oversees BuzzSumo's content and public relations, and is invested in helping practitioners get the absolute most out of their strategies.

#FuturePRoof: Edition Six

CHAPTER
18

CHAPTER **18**

PROPHET

Aaron Kwittken | Developer

PRophet uses AI to help modern practitioners become more performative, productive and predictive by generating, analysing and testing content that predicts earned media interest and sentiment.

PRophet is the first generative and predictive AI SaaS platform built by and for modern public relations and marketing practitioners. Using a combination of natural language processing and machine learning, PRophet assesses a reporter's past coverage to predict the level of interest in a specific topic or angle. As a result, PRophet prevents practitioners from having to weed through hundreds, if not thousands, of random names in a traditional media database search query.

The tool is designed to help communicators become more performative, predictive and productive. The innovative platform eliminates the guesswork, using the PRophet dataset and technology to guide public relations practitioners toward greater success in not only achieving coverage of an announcement but in developing a positive, lasting relationship with the journalist by delivering more relevant content on a more consistent basis.

In March 2023, PRophet launched Taylor - the communications industry's first generative AI writing tool. Fully integrated into the PRophet platform and built on top of OpenAI, Taylor enables brands and agencies to create compelling content more efficiently than ever before and provides insights into which types of content are most effective.

Its functionality is simple: users provide a short prompt or full press release, and Taylor produces a pitch in under two minutes. Taylor can rewrite releases, too - another iteration that takes just a few seconds to generate. The AI can redraft a multitude of times over, allowing users to move forward with the new copy or edit and apply a human touch to the original. The same process can be used to create blog posts, articles, social media content and more at the same speed.

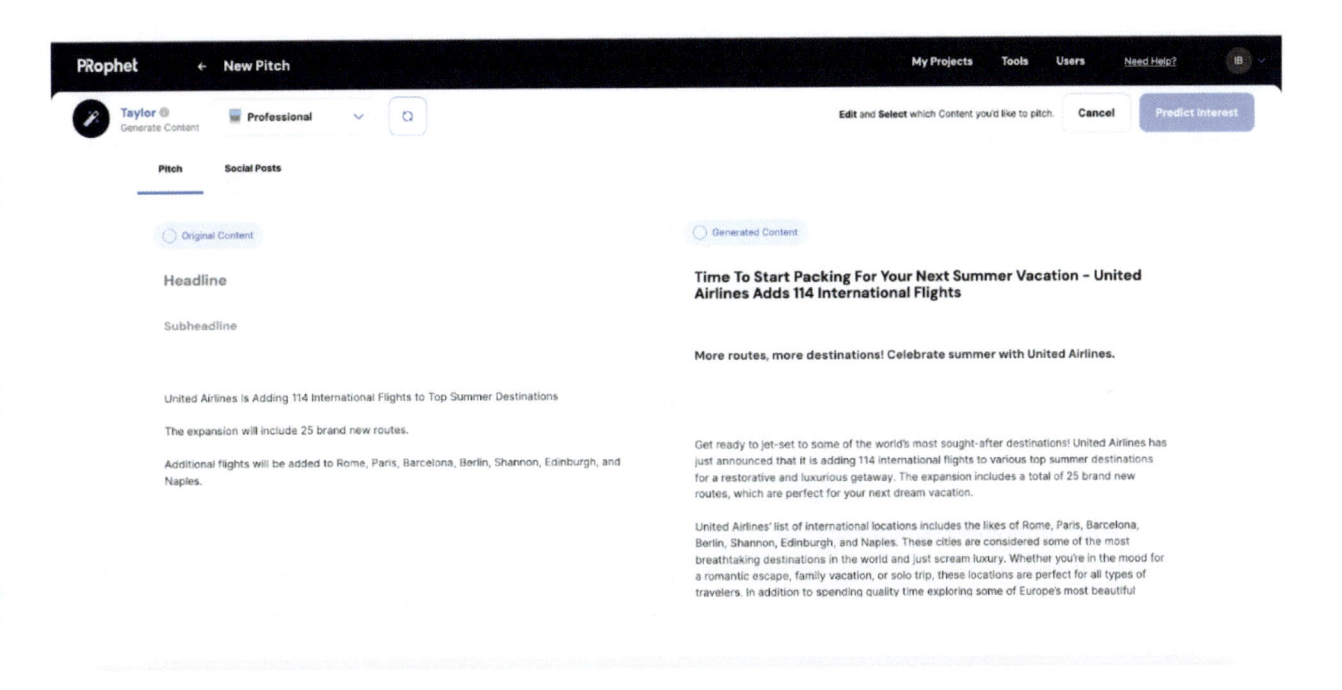

The tool offers the choice of tone for generated content - persuasive, professional, luxury, friendly, bold, adventurous and more. Once PRophet's predictive AI analyses the text and compiles a list of reporters for outreach, Taylor will then personalise pitches for any reporter users select. From there, users can accept the pitch, edit what Taylor provided or ask it to rewrite the pitch again.

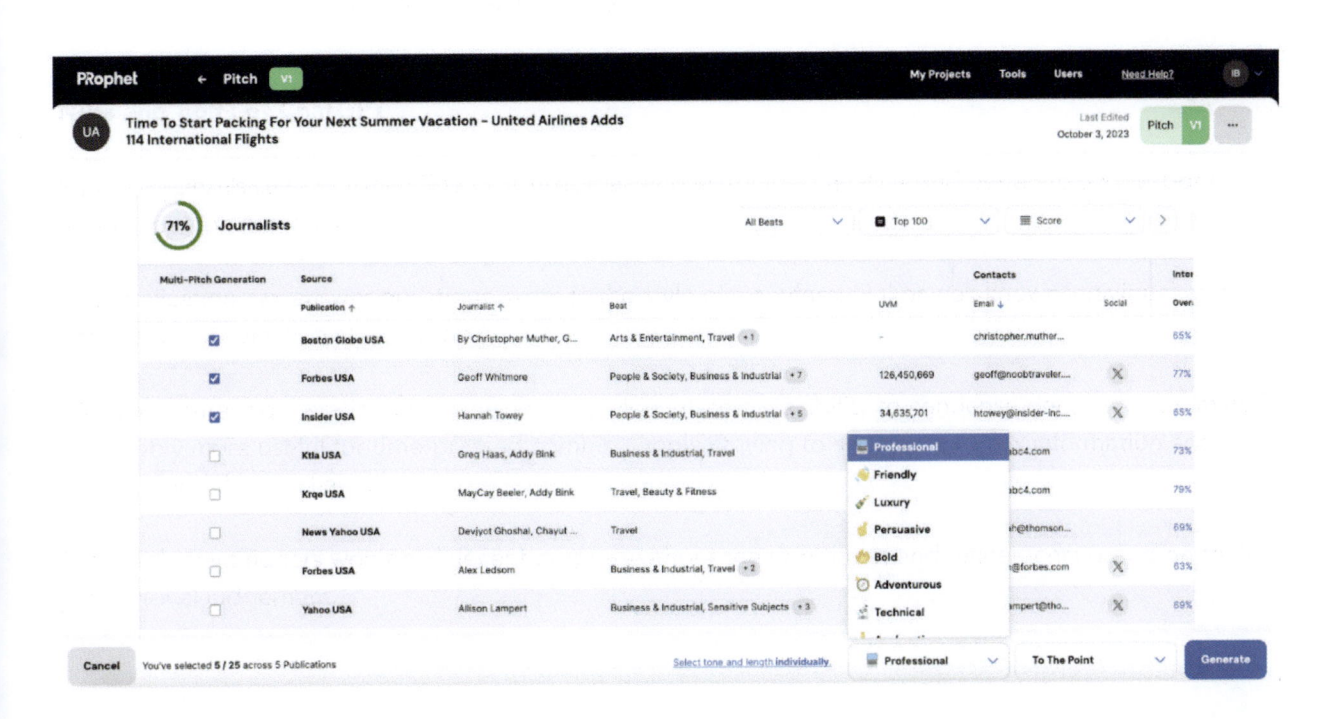

In July 2023, PRophet launched two new features powered by generative AI, a Multi-Pitch Generator and a Bio Generator tool. The new Multi-Pitch feature allows enterprise users to generate and further personalise pitches for up to 25 reporters in under three minutes. Users have the option to choose different length pitches as well as tone preferences. The Bio Generator also uses AI to generate an executive biography in seconds by inputting a LinkedIn URL.

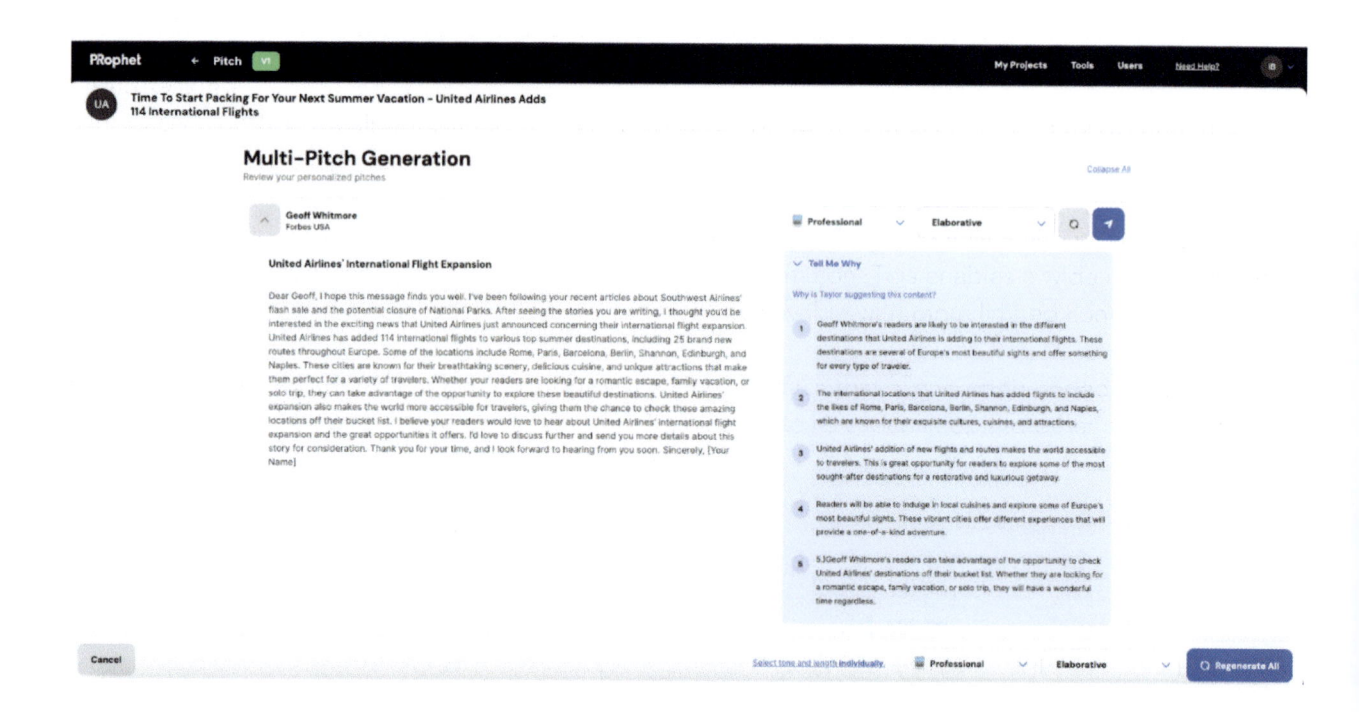

In October 2023, PRophet expanded into AI-driven influencer marketing and news monitoring, and unveiled new platform branding – PRophet Earn, Influence and Monitor. PRophet has integrated Koalifyed Influencer Marketing Platform which builds and deploys brand-specific influencer marketing programs. PRophet and PeakMetrics have come together to create Monitor for personalised media alerts and help brands fight misinformation and disinformation online. With Earn, users have access to the full suite of existing media relations tools.

Aaron Kwittken, founder and CEO, PRophet, CEO, Stagwell Marketing Cloud Comms Tech Business Unit
https://www.linkedin.com/in/aaronkwittken/

Aaron Kwittken is the CEO of Stagwel Marketing Cloud's Comms Tech Business Unit, a proprietary suite of SaaS products built for in-house marketers. He is also the founder and CEO of PRophet and founder of Stagwell brand KWT Global where he currently serves as chairman.

#FuturePRoof: Edition Six

CHAPTER

19

CHAPTER **19**

PROWLY

Aleksandra Kubicka | Developer

Prowly is a public relations management tool that helps public relations practitioners earn media coverage through creative storytelling, personalisation and innovative technology.

Users can foster long-term relationships with journalists by drafting effective strategies based on industry data and prove their value to clients and stakeholders with easy-to-understand insights from media monitoring. This all-in-one media relations platform has recently implemented AI into the whole process of creating and sending press releases.

Where it fits within the public relations workflow

Prowly is optimising how public relations practitioners work with AI and has created a solution that assists during routine activities by igniting the creative process. It helps specifically where public relations practitioners experience the biggest obstacles:

- Starting the draft of a press release.
- Crafting clear messaging.
- Preparing a quote from the company's representative.
- Expanding media lists in new topic areas.
- Writing an email pitch with a catchy subject line.

Prowly made using AI accessible with already-made prompts, so users don't need to do it alone and go through trial and error with what works and what doesn't. The AI algorithms are trained to not act like a simple writing tool but like a writer with years of experience in public relations. Rules, word limitations, guidelines, outlines - you name it.

Drafting a press release with AI

To start drafting with AI, the user chooses the type of press release, defines the audience and writes three key messages. Then, replies to ten live-generated questions related to the input provided. The conversational interface extracts relevant information and asks questions that the journalist would ask. By answering them, the user can ensure that the final material is of higher quality, contains facts and figures, and proof points to the key messages. It also helps to uncover new aspects and details that may be relevant for journalists and tweak the messaging.

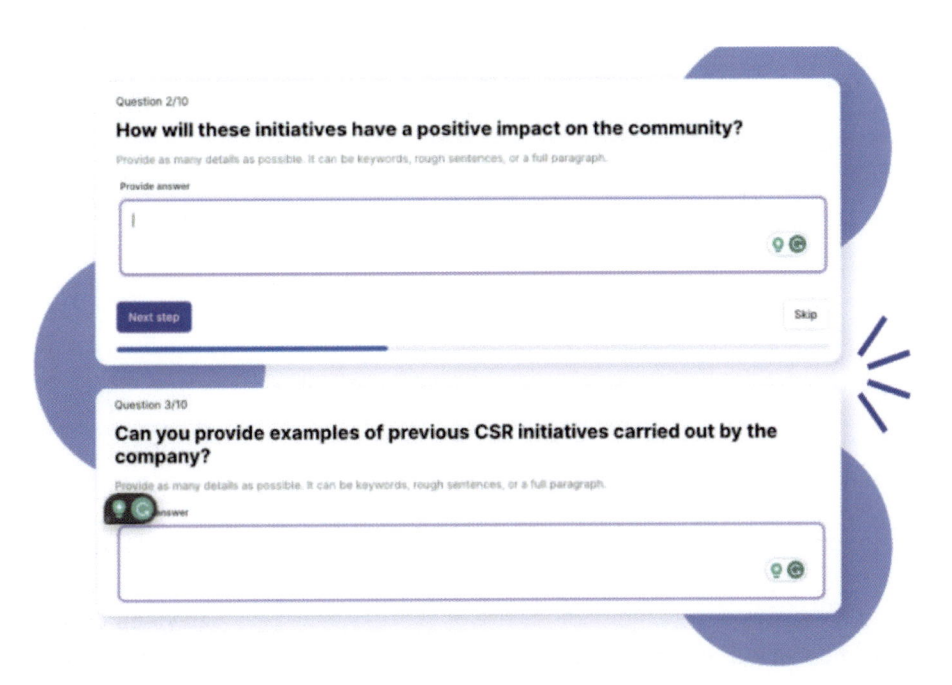

The outcome is a comprehensive draft with an informative quote from the company's representative, serving as a strong foundation for the final press release. Prowly's AI Press Release Creator is available in American and British English, Spanish, French, German, Portuguese, and Polish.

Content-based contact recommendations

Once a press release is ready, the tool initiates the journalist discovery process. By analysing its content and keywords, it identifies the ideal media contacts. It allows playing around with the keywords and discovering new targeting possibilities. Users expand the range of recommendations, testing various angles.

Combining AI with a media database with over one million records allows for quicker discovery of new media outlets worth pitching to, including niche ones. Practitioners can save hours on manual searches and building media lists for different story angles. Prowly helps to initiate long-lasting relationships through proper email personalisation and knowing who to pitch.

Drafting emails to journalists

Based on the attached press release, AI will generate a preliminary pitch. It will include four key messages in bullet points, exactly how journalists like it. Easy to quickly scan with clear newsworthy parts. Users can regenerate the content to make it shorter or longer, ensuring it matches perfectly with their pitching strategies.

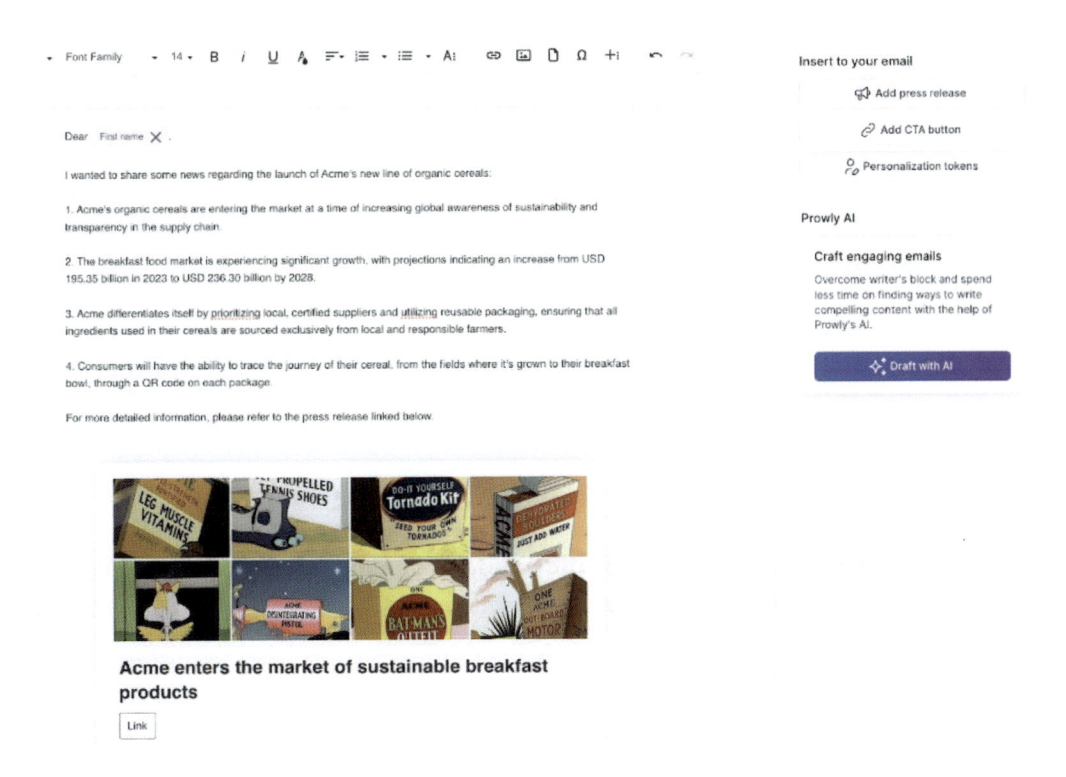

AI will generate ideas for catchy subject lines, crucial to increasing open rates. The Prowly tool also provides suggestions for the preview text, an extension of the subject line visible in the journalist's inbox. It is a small yet important element that practitioners often overlook. It's worth it to use both hooks to grab the attention with the right keywords.

Use cases

Prowly AI was designed to assist public practitioners of all experience levels and from any type of organisation. The entire AI-enhanced workflow takes place on one platform without purchasing different tools for each step or prompting generative AI that is not trained for storytelling. Practitioners can accelerate their workflow and focus on what matters most in the media relations game: pitch quality and relations with journalists.

Aleksandra Kubicka, public relations evangelist, Prowly
https://www.linkedin.com/in/aleksandrakubicka/

Aleksandra is a public relations evangelist at Prowly, with 14 years of experience in public relations and business-to-business communication. She has worked in public relations agencies, startups, and in-house teams of global brands and is passionate about using technology, AI and advanced analytics to enhance storytelling.

CHAPTER 20

CHAPTER **20**

ONEPITCH

Sarah Pekala | Practitioner

OnePitch utilises AI to optimise the public relations pitching process by helping create targeted media lists, providing feedback to improve pitch quality, and tracking interactions, saving time and boosting pitch success.

Every public relations practitioner at an agency or solo publicist can attest that researching journalists, creating media lists and crafting unique pitches make up a large percentage of their work. Grabbing a journalist's attention with a compelling pitch is also getting more challenging. We're constantly competing for their time and attention in their inboxes. One of my favourite tools for public relations practitioners is OnePitch.

OnePitch is a SaaS tool that aims to connect the right journalists to the right pitches. OnePitch helps media relations practitioners across the pitching process find relevant journalists, craft the perfect pitch and track that pitch's success.

Find relevant journalists

The ability to create unlimited media lists is a game-changer for public relations practitioners in an agency environment like mine. I represent up to seven clients simultaneously across many different industries. I'm juggling at least seven different media lists at any given time, which takes time to create and update regularly. OnePitch creates custom media lists with journalists' email, social profiles, recent articles and resources. I also receive a match score, which tells me with a percentage point how closely their beat matches my needs.

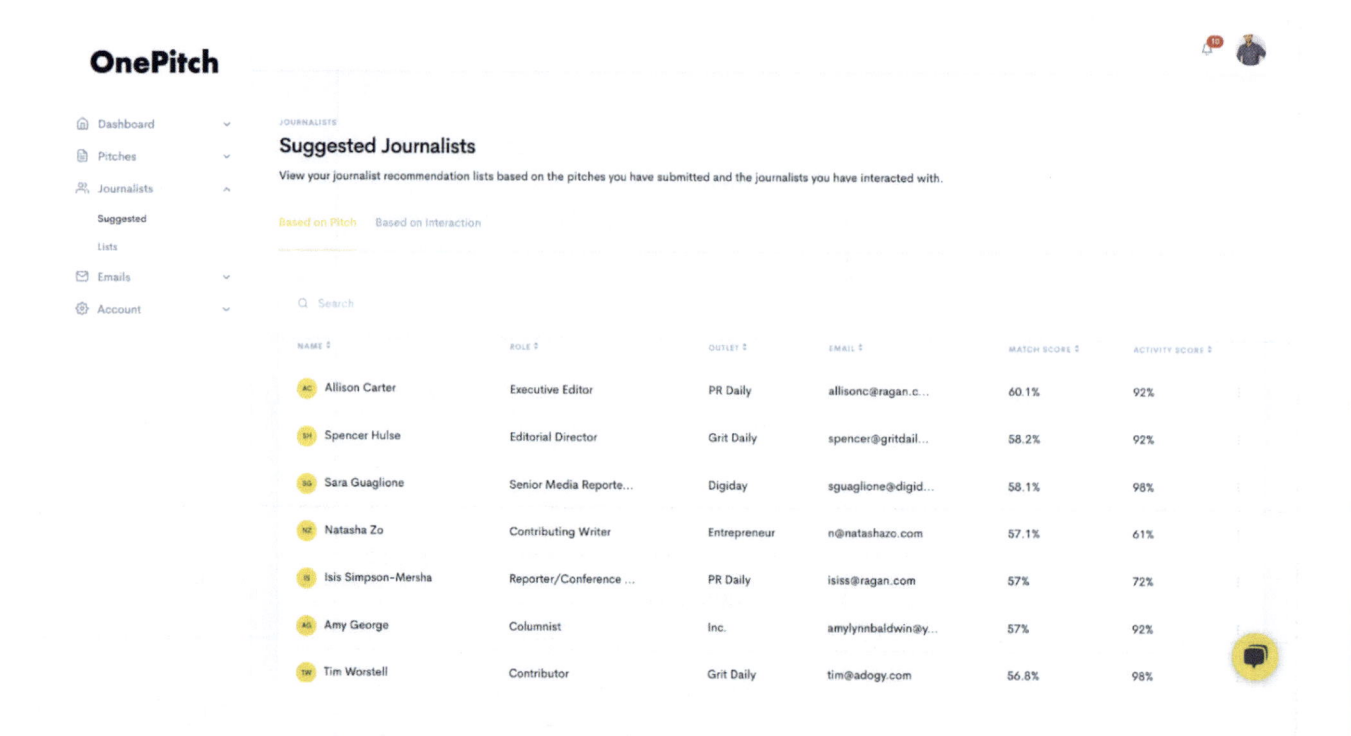

Drafting a pitch

Once I have my target media list, crafting a pitch is where the art of public relations begins. Sure, I could use ChatGPT to help me write a targeted pitch, but I often find the results too generic. OnePitch's Pitch Checker tool shows me exactly which essential elements are missing. I enter information on what exactly the pitch is, why my pitch is newsworthy and the subject line, and it uses AI to calculate my pitch score and guides me based on journalist feedback. It helps me understand if my subject line is too long, whether my pitch feels too promotional or has the right amount of context. Then OnePitch gives me a list of journalists that match, saving me tons of time manually going through my lists.

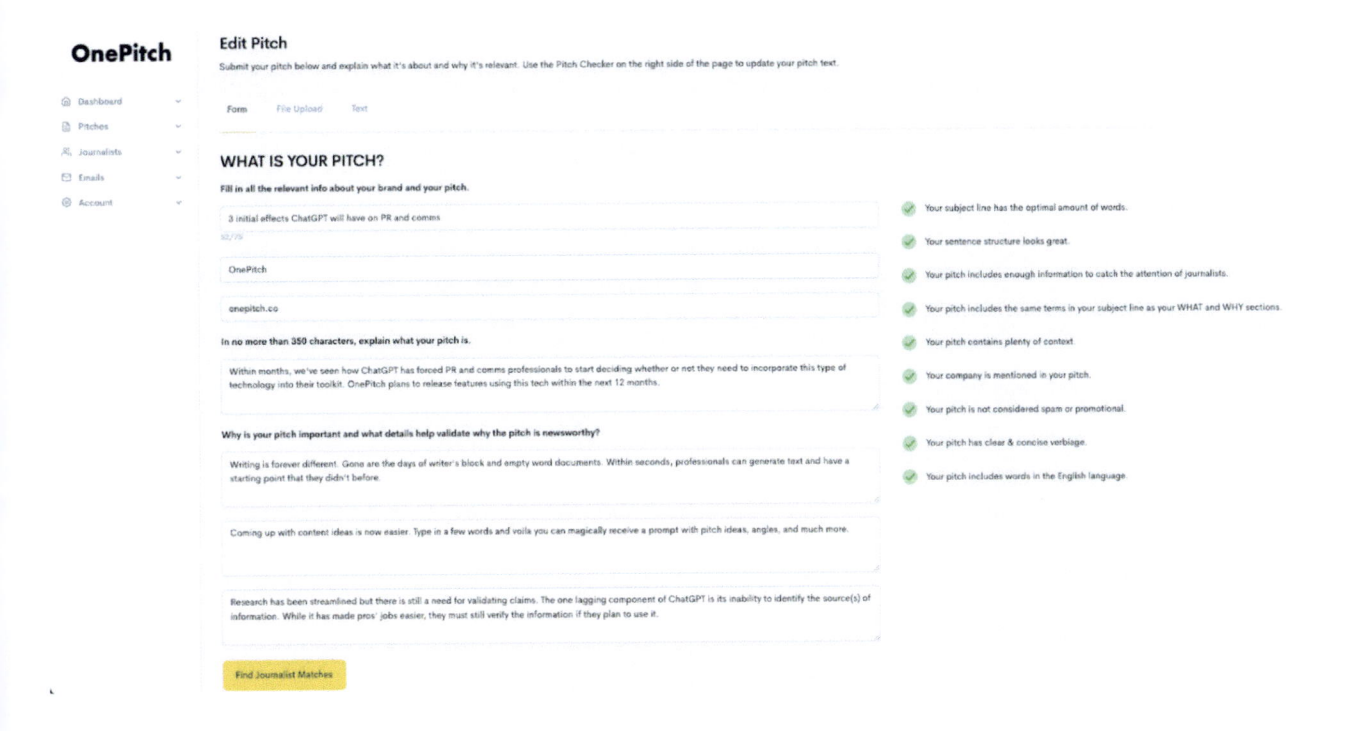

Tracking the success of a pitch

What makes OnePitch unique is that not only does it help me write better pitches, but it also helps me track a pitch after I click 'send.' Because I can send my pitches directly through the tool, it collects data like email opens, clicks and responses on the app. This data is key for knowing how my pitch landed with the journalists. If they open it four times in 24 hours, for instance, that's usually a good sign that they may be interested. It can be hard to keep track of every single interaction you've had with a journalist daily. I can track every interaction by sending all my pitches through OnePitch vs. in my email directly, giving me better data for reporting to my clients.

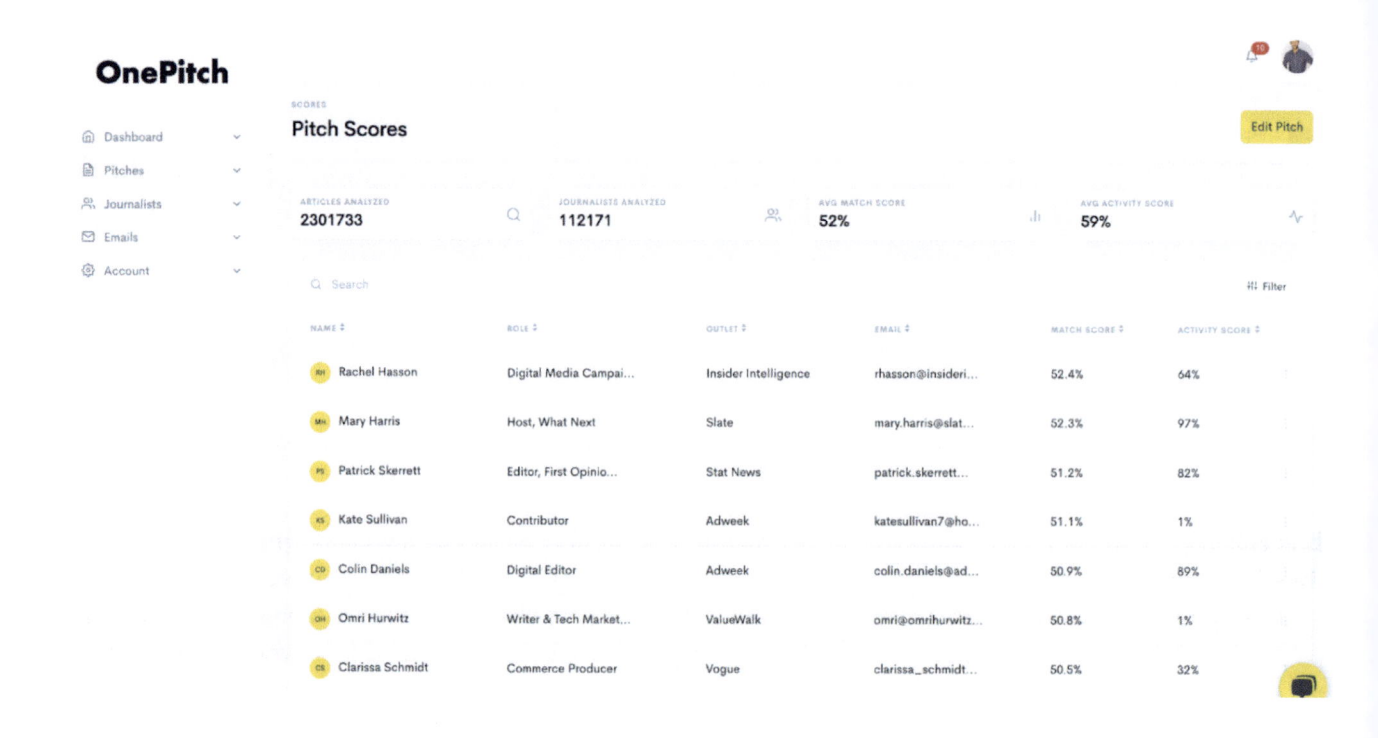

OnePitch has a free version, but it's limited. The free instance of OnePitch allows you to write one pitch, get up to 10 journalist matches for the pitch and create one media list; all fine if you're an internal communications lead at a company with one big announcement moment or data to pitch. But OnePitch shines once you sign up for the unlimited subscription, which gives you access to all their features for $50 per month — well worth what you get from it. Beyond the inexpensive price, their customer support and educational materials are a huge plus. Their brand creates helpful podcasts, articles, and Twitter content, building community amongst its users.

Sarah Pekala, senior account director, BAM
https://www.linkedin.com/in/sarah-pekala/

Sarah Pekala is a senior account director at BAM, a public relations and communications agency that moves stories forward for venture-backed startups and venture funds that challenge, change, and create entire industries. Before BAM, Sarah was content marketing lead for multiple VC-backed startups, focusing on executive thought leadership and corporate communications.

#FuturePRoof: Edition Six

CHAPTER
21

CHAPTER **21**

PROPEL

Zach Cutler | Developer

Propel is a leading AI-powered Public Relations Management (PRM) tool. Propel enables agencies and in-house teams to generate content, discover media targets, pitch stories, monitor coverage/ROI and win at earned media. Features include a full CRM for media relations, Gmail and Outlook plugins, a generative AI powered suite, media monitoring service, and business outcomes indicator.

Where it fits within public relations workflow

Propel PRM fits into every part of the public relations workflow, from finding journalists to pitch to showing how well campaigns are going - both in terms of coverage and bottom line. The PRM manages the entire flow from pitch to publish; from gen AI pitch and press release writers and media list management to sales funnel metrics resulting from successful placements in publications. Propel's platform can touch every piece of the typical communications workflow, streamline it, and make it more organised. In short, it automates and simplifies the mundane, time consuming aspects of media relations practice so that practitioners can focus on messaging, play down strategy, and build journalist relationships.

How to use it

Using Propel is quite straightforward depending on what the objective is. To use the gen AI pitch, press release, and article writer, all a public relations practitioner needs to do is prompt the AI to get it to write a draft of what they want. Communicators can also input a draft pitch to get the AI to make a media list for them.

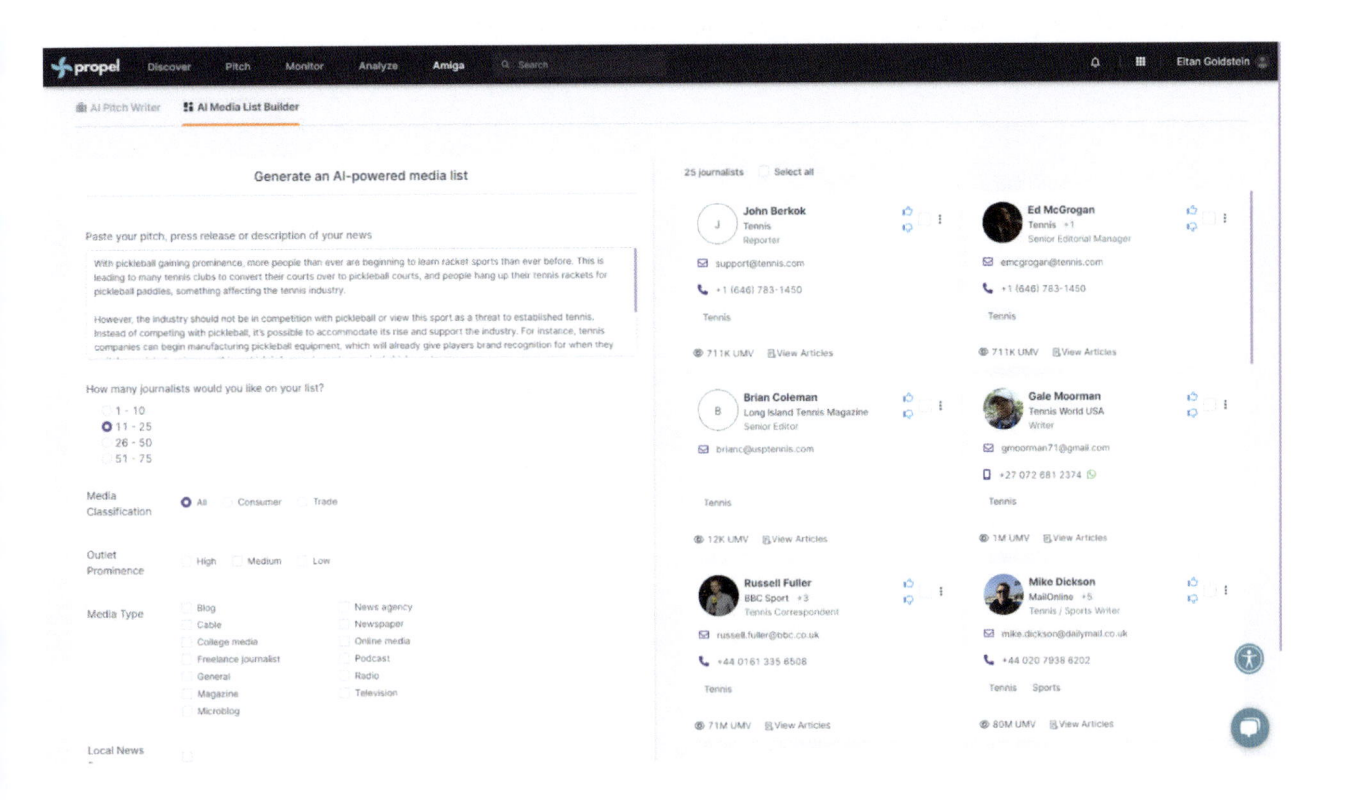

Propel's journalist database is augmented by AI which can tell a media relations practitioner everything from what topics a journalist writes about, to open and response rates and even what day of the week and time they're most likely to open a pitch. Communicators also have the option to create or add these journalists to media lists manually, as well as upload pre-made CSVs into the system.

To send a pitching campaign, all one needs to do is pull up the relevant media list inside their Gmail or Outlook, and then go through the list to determine who gets sent what. Upon hitting the PitchBooster button, the emails get saved to drafts, enabling communicators to tailor each pitch to each journalist.

Once the pitch is sent, it's automatically logged in the "story funnel." As journalists begin asking for information, communicators can move the journalist tile along the funnel until the story is published. They can also write notes on the tile so everyone in the team can see if there are any special instructions.

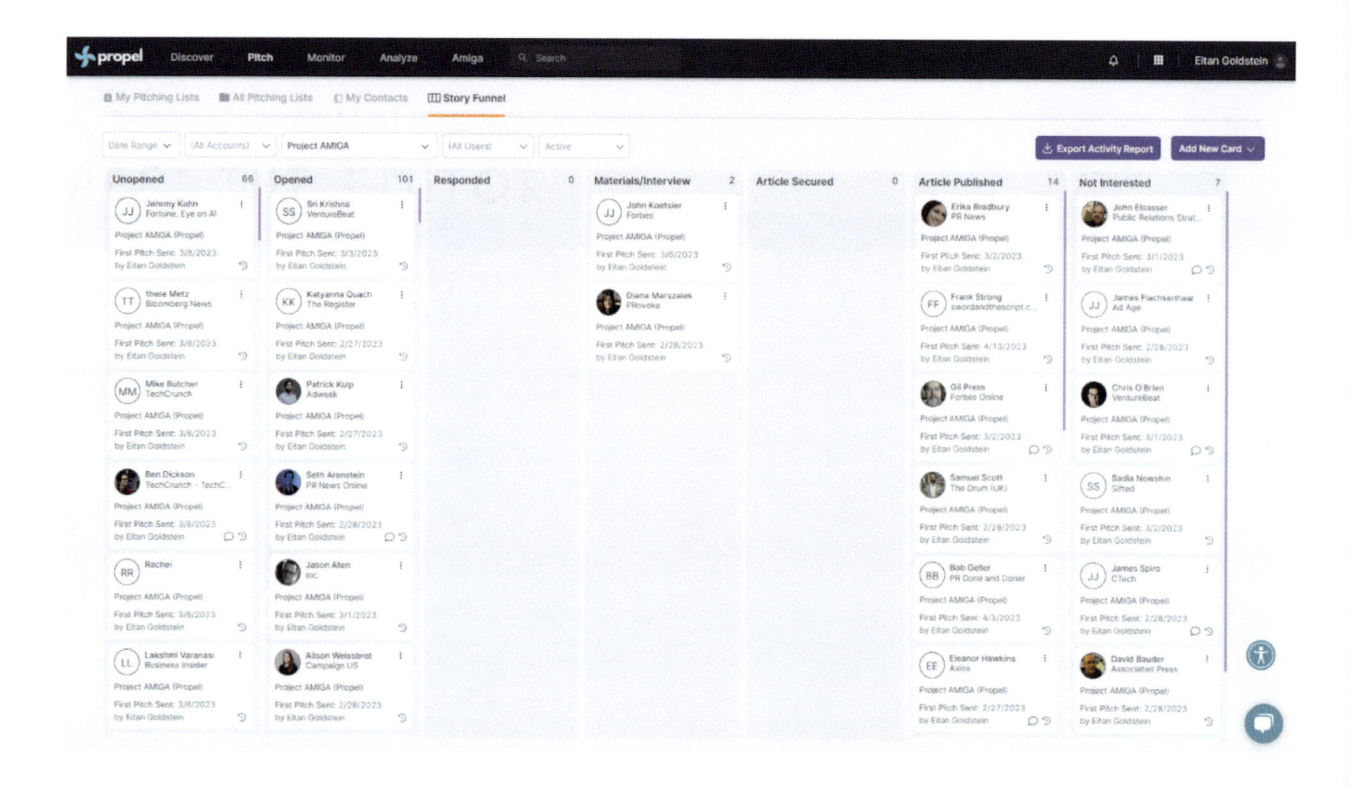

Finally, upon publication, the practitioner inputs the link to the story and Propel is automatically able to find the unique monthly visitors, title, author, etc of the article. This then ties into the organisation's conversion metrics, enabling the organisation to see how many people enter their sales funnel from a particular piece of coverage.

Example use case

The best use case for the product is us! Our in-house public relations team uses the PRM every day to gain earned media coverage for the company, and averages over 20 pieces of coverage per quarter. Propel has consistently been surpassing all its competitors in terms of media coverage for over a year. This has been driving brand awareness and sales.

Zach Cutler, CEO, Propel
https://www.linkedin.com/in/zachc

Zach Cutler is the CEO of the fully accessible public relations platform Propel PRM and is one of the only VC-backed tech founders with a physical disability. Prior to this he owned and operated his own public relations agency - Cutler PR - for nine years and was the agency of record in the US for 70 tech start-ups.

MEET THE EDITOR

Stephen Waddington

Stephen Waddington is the founder and managing partner of Wadds Inc., a professional advisory firm that helps agencies and communications teams with planning, strategic decision-making, and execution. He is also the co-founder of Socially Mobile, a not-for-profit PR training school helping those lower socio-economic backgrounds and under-represented groups to increase their earning potential.

A PhD research student at Leeds Business School studying public relations and management, he is a former President of the CIPR and has written and edited more than ten books about public relations practice, including Exploring PR and Management Communication, published by Pearson in January 2021.

Stephen was previously managing director at Metia Group (2019-2020), an international digital marketing agency. He was Chief Engagement Officer at Ketchum (2012-2018), an Omnicom-owned agency responsible for integrating digital and social capabilities in client engagements across the agency's international network.

Stephen originally trained as an engineer and a journalist before pursuing a public relations career. He co-founded, managed and sold two award-winning public relations agencies, Rainier PR in 1998 and Speed in 2009. He is a Chartered PR Practitioner, a CIPR Fellow (Hon), a PRCA Fellow, a member of the IoD, and a member of the IPRA.

If you're interested in exploring issues raised by this latest edition of #FuturePRoof within your organisation through workshops, training or rethinking your workflow, you can contact Stephen at: **Stephen.Waddington@wadds.co.uk.**

Printed in Great Britain
by Amazon